GREEK COOKING

Traditional Recipes

by the celebrated chef T. Tolis

EKDOTIKE ATHENON S.A.

Athens 2009

Recipes - preparation and presentation of recipes: **Tasos Tolis,**
Chief Chef at the Astir Hotel, Vouliagmeni, graduate of the
Parnitha School of Tourist Trades, postgraduate study in Lausanne,
Switzerland.

Publisher: **Christiana G. Christopoulou**

Edited by: **Myrto Stavropoulou**
Translation: **Gafe Fox-Sofianou**
Art Director: **Tonia Kotsoni**
Supervision of photography: **Anastasia Michael**
Photography: **Dimitris Benetos**
Phototypesetting: **Photosyn ABEE**
Colour seperation, printing and binding:
Metron S.A.-Ekdotike Hellados

CONTENTS

INDEX

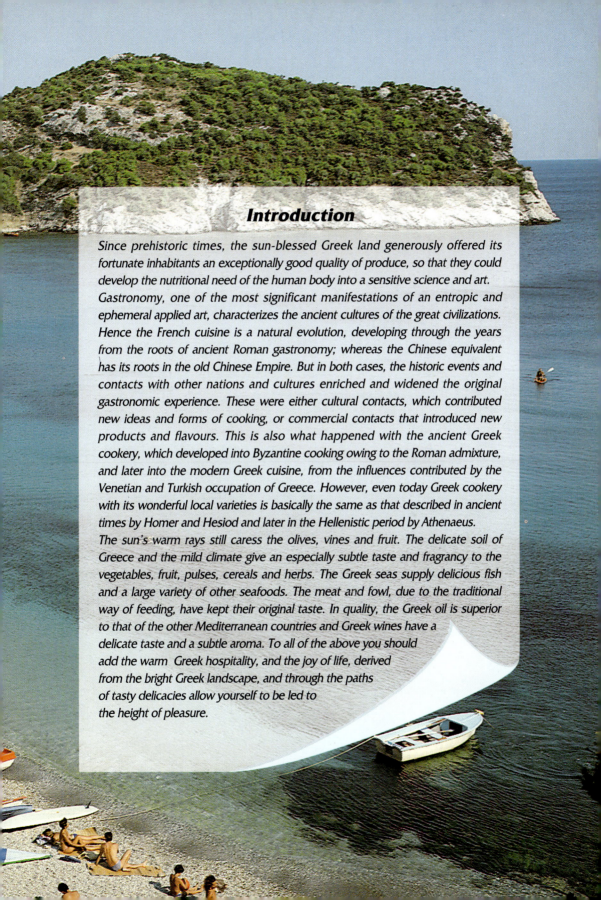

Introduction

Since prehistoric times, the sun-blessed Greek land generously offered its fortunate inhabitants an exceptionally good quality of produce, so that they could develop the nutritional need of the human body into a sensitive science and art. Gastronomy, one of the most significant manifestations of an entropic and ephemeral applied art, characterizes the ancient cultures of the great civilizations. Hence the French cuisine is a natural evolution, developing through the years from the roots of ancient Roman gastronomy; whereas the Chinese equivalent has its roots in the old Chinese Empire. But in both cases, the historic events and contacts with other nations and cultures enriched and widened the original gastronomic experience. These were either cultural contacts, which contributed new ideas and forms of cooking, or commercial contacts that introduced new products and flavours. This is also what happened with the ancient Greek cookery, which developed into Byzantine cooking owing to the Roman admixture, and later into the modern Greek cuisine, from the influences contributed by the Venetian and Turkish occupation of Greece. However, even today Greek cookery with its wonderful local varieties is basically the same as that described in ancient times by Homer and Hesiod and later in the Hellenistic period by Athenaeus.

The sun's warm rays still caress the olives, vines and fruit. The delicate soil of Greece and the mild climate give an especially subtle taste and fragrancy to the vegetables, fruit, pulses, cereals and herbs. The Greek seas supply delicious fish and a large variety of other seafoods. The meat and fowl, due to the traditional way of feeding, have kept their original taste. In quality, the Greek oil is superior to that of the other Mediterranean countries and Greek wines have a delicate taste and a subtle aroma. To all of the above you should add the warm Greek hospitality, and the joy of life, derived from the bright Greek landscape, and through the paths of tasty delicacies allow yourself to be led to the height of pleasure.

Starters

Dolmades yialandzi

Stuffed vine leaves

Ingredients for 6 persons

(Attica)

40 (tender young) vine leaves
1 teacup rice
1 teacup oil
2-3 spring onions finely
    chopped
dill, mint,
salt, pepper

Fry the spring onions in half the oil. Add the rice and cook slowly for a few minutes. Add the dill, mint, salt and pepper, and a little water, and leave to cook for 5 minutes. Set aside to cool. Wash the vine leaves well, and scald in boiling water. Place a small amount of the cooled mixture onto each vine leaf and wrap into parcels. Put the dolmades in rows in a pan, add the lemon juice and a little water. Simmer gently for about an hour. Stuffed vine leaves are served cold.

Spetzofai

Village sausages with red pepper and tomato

Ingredients for 4 persons

(Pilion)

1 kilo village sausages
2 onions
2 red peppers
1-2 tomatoes
1 clove garlic
2-3 tablespoons olive oil

Heat the oil until it becomes hot, add the sliced onions and fry until they become transparent, add the sausages, red peppers, garlic and the finely chopped tomatoes. Cook for 15-20 minutes and serve at once.

Stuffed vine leaves, top
Village sausages with red pepper and tomato, bottom
Little cheese pies, centre right
Manouri cheese with quince preserve, centre left

Tiropittakia

Little cheese pies

Ingredients for 6 persons.

(Mitilinil)

350 gr. Feta cheese
100 gr. cheese
  (Kefalograviera)
2 eggs
300 gr. filo pastry
1 teacup melted butter
white pepper
finely chopped parsley

Crumble the Feta cheese into a bowl, add the grated Kefalograviera cheese, parsley, eggs, white pepper and mix well. Cut the filo pastry into strips 6x25 cms. Brush the melted butter onto the pastry, and place a teaspoon of the mixture onto each strip. Fold the pastry forming a triangular parcel. Place the cheese pies on a buttered baking pan, brush the pie tops with butter, and bake on a moderate oven for about 15 minutes. Serve them hot.

Manouri me kidoni

Manouri cheese with quince preserve

Ingredients for 4 persons

(Trikala)

800 gr. Manouri cheese
1 teacup flour
2 eggs beaten
4 tablespoons quince preserve
frying oil

Cut the cheese into small sticks. Flour the sticks, dip into the beaten egg and fry in hot oil on both sides. Serve slightly warm (not hot) with quince preserve.

Fried cheese

Saganaki me kefalograviera

Fried cheese

Ingredients for 4-6 persons

(Arta)

**6 portions of cheese
(Kefalograviera)
1 teacup flour
2-3 eggs (beaten)
1-2 lemons
frying oil**

Put the oil to heat in a frying pan, taking care that it does not get too hot. Dip the cheese pieces into water, coat them in flour and then dip them into the beaten egg. Fry the cheese on both sides until they become golden brown. Serve hot with lemon.

Kolokythokeftedes

Fried courgette/zucchini balls

Ingredients for six persons

(Githion)

1 kilo courgettes (fairly large)
2-3 onions
2 eggs (beaten)
2-3 tablespoons toasted bread
crumbs (rusks)
2 teacups flour
2-3 tablespoons grated
Feta cheese
oil for frying
mint, parsley
salt and pepper

Grate the courgettes on the grater and leave them to drain very well. Place them in a basin and add the beaten eggs, grated Feta cheese and onions, finely chopped parsley and mint. Season with salt and pepper and add the toasted bread crumbs a little at a time. Put the oil in the frying pan to heat. Take a spoonful of the mixture and shape into balls, coat them with flour and place them one at a time into the hot oil in the frying pan. Leave the balls until they become golden brown. Remove and drain on kitchen paper, and serve them hot.

Taramokeftedes

Fish roe balls

Ingredients for six persons

(Pilion)

230 gr. fish roe (tarama)
350 gr. wet bread crumbs
5 tablespoons flour
frying oil
finely chopped parsley, dill
and mint
½ grated onion
pepper

Soak the fish roe in water overnight to remove the salt. Fry the onions well in a little oil. In a bowl knead together the fish roe, bread crumbs, parsley, dill, mint, onion, pepper and the flour until the mixture becomes a stiff dough. Form into balls and fry in hot oil. Drain and serve them hot.

Fried courgette/zucchini balls
Fish roe balls
Potato balls
Chickpea balls

Patatokeftedes

Potato balls

Ingredients for 6 persons

(Paramithia)

1 kilo potatoes
2-3 eggs
3-4 dessertspoons grated
Feta cheese
frying oil
flour
mint, parsley
salt, pepper

Boil the potatoes, strain and mash them. Add to the potatoes the parsley, mint, Feta and beaten eggs. Mix the ingredients well and form into small balls. Flour the balls and fry them in hot oil on both sides. Drain well and serve.

Revithokeftedes

Chickpea balls

Ingredients for 6 persons

(Dodecanese)

1 kilo chickpeas
500 gr. mashed potato
1 medium finely chopped
  onion
2 eggs (beaten)
1 dessertspoon oregano
frying oil
flour
salt and pepper

Soak the chickpeas over night, then boil them for fifty minutes. Strain and mash. Place the mashed chickpeas in a bowl together with the mashed potatoes, beaten eggs, finely chopped onion, flour, oregano salt and pepper. Mix the ingredients well, then form it into small balls. Flour the balls and fry in hot oil until they are golden brown on both sides.

Bacaliaros skordalia

Cod with garlic sauce

Ingredients for 6 persons

(Ithaki)

1 kilo salted dry cod
1 teacup flour
1 teacup water
1-2 eggs
frying oil
white pepper

Cut the cod into small pieces and soak in water overnight, changing the water 2-3 times. Whilst draining the fish, prepare the batter. In a bowl, mix the flour, water, beaten eggs and pepper. Dip the pieces of cod in the batter, one at a time, place in the hot oil and fry. Serve with garlie sauce (see Skordalia in salad recipes).

Cod with garlic sauce, bottom left
Garlic sauce, top left
Mussels with tomato sauce and garlic, bottom right

Mydia me tomata kai skordo

Mussels with tomato and garlic

Ingredients for 4 to 6 persons

(Kavala)

1 kilo mussels
3-4 cloves of garlic
2-3 tomatoes
2-3 dessertspoons oil
1 glass of white wine
parsley
salt, pepper

Wash the mussels thoroughly. In a frying pan, brown the garlic in the oil, add the mussels and stir well. Pour in the wine, then add the finely chopped tomatoes, the parsley and season with the desired salt and pepper. Boil for 20 minutes. Serve the mussels warm with fresh parsley

Chtapodi ladorigani

Octopus with oil and oregano

Ingredients for 6 persons

(Cyclades)

**1 kilo octopus
1 teacup olive oil
½ teacup vinegar
oregano
salt, pepper**

Wash the octopus and remove ink bag. Place the octopus in a saucepan with the vinegar and a little water. Bring to the boil and simmer until it is tender. Cut the octopus into small bite size pieces and add salt. Beat the oil and vinegar with the oregano, pour over the octopus and serve.

Taramosalata

Fish roe salad

Ingredients for 6 persons

(Kavala)

**300 gr. fish roe
1 kilo peeled potatoes
200 grms. wet bread crumbs
1 teacup olive oil
½ teacup sunflower oil
juice of 2 lemons
1 finely grated onion
drops of vinegar
parsley and some olives**

Boil the potatoes and mash them, then add the bread crumbs. In a mortar, pound the onion with the fish roe, continue pounding whilst adding the potato puree, bread crumbs and lemon juice. Gradually add both kinds of oil at the same time, stirring continuously, until the salad thickens. Add the drops of vinegar and stirr. Garnish with parsley and olives.

Volvi me ladoxido

Small onion bulbs with oil and vinegar

(Crete)

Ingredients for 6 persons

1 kilo of small onions (bulbs)
2 small glasses of wine vinegar
2-3 tablespoons olive oil
dill
salt and pepper

Clean the onions and boil in a little water with half the vinegar for 15-20 minutes. Beat the oil with the rest of the vinegar and add the salt, pepper and finely chopped dill. Strain the onions, pour over the oil and vinegar and serve.

Tsiri me ladoxido

Dried mackerel with oil and vinegar

(Naxos)

These small dried fish can be prepared in two ways:

1. Grilled and made into a salad with oil and vinegar.

2. Beat the backbone to make the dried mackerel flat, and cut off the head. Make a batter with water and flour, coat the fish and fry in hot oil. This is always accompanied with garlic sauce (see Skordalia in Salad recipes) and tomato salad.

Octopus with oil and oregano
Fish roe salad, bottom right
Onion bulbs with oil and vinegar, top right ▶

Marides tiganites

Fried whitebait

Ingredients for 6 persons

(Attiki)

1 kilo whitebait
1 teacup flour
2 lemons
salt

Wash the whitebait well and strain in a colander. Heat the oil well, in a deep frying pan. Flour the whitebait, shake to remove the excess flour, and fry them until they become golden brown. Serve hot, with fresh lemon.

Kalamarakia tiganita

Fried squid

Ingredients for 6 persons

(Preveza)

1 kilo squid
flour
lemon, parsley
frying oil
salt

Clean the squid and rub them with salt. Dip them in flour and place them one by one to fry in plenty of hot oil until they become golden brown. Take them out with a perforated spoon, add salt and serve them garnished with lemon and parsley.

Fried whitebait, bottom
Fried squid, top

Gardoumba

Ingredients for 10 persons

1 lamb's liver (and kidney)
1 lamb's intestines
2-3 spring onions
olive oil
oregano, dill
salt, pepper

Parcels of lamb's liver and kidney wrapped in intestines

(Kalambaka)

Turn the intestines inside out, wash them very well and sprinkle with lemon juice. Wash the liver and kidneys and cut into long strips. Place the offal on small wooden skewers. Take about 20-30 cms. of the intestines and wrap it around some strips of liver and kidney, adding a little chopped spring onion to each parcel (gardoumba). Remove the skewers and place the gardoumbes (or parcels) in a small baking pan. Season with salt and pepper, oregano, finely chopped dill and pour over the oil. Bake in a preheated oven for approximately one hour on 220° C, turning them to brown on both sides. Serve hot with strained yoghourt.

Kokoretsi

Ingredients for 6 to 8 persons

1 kilo of lamb's entrails
2 lamb's intestines
grated goat's cheese
    (Kefalotyri)
olive oil, oregano
salt, pepper
1 lemon (juice)
some lettuce leaves

Lamb's intestines

(Roumeli)

Turn the intestines inside out and wash them very well. Cut the entrails into small square pieces, wash them well and drain. Place them in a bowl and sprinkle with the desired salt, pepper, oregano and grated cheese and pour over a little oil.

Place on a small skewer in succession the pieces of liver - lungs - heart - fat and testicles until all the pieces have been used up. Wrap the intestines around the offal and cook on the spit or in the oven, basting with a mixture of oil and lemon. Remove the skewer, cut into slices and serve with lettuce leaves and fresh oregano.

Parcels of lamb's liver and kidney wrapped in intestines, bottom
Lamb's intestines, top

Fava

Split yellow peas

Ingredients for 4 persons

(Santorini)

500 gr. yellow peas
2-3 onions
2-3 lemons
oil, parsley
salt

Wash the peas and boil, skim off the froth continuously. Add the onions, cut into quarters and leave to boil for one hour. Mash the peas into a purée, then add the salt and oil and stir continuously for 10 minutes. Fava can be served hot or cold with finely chopped onion, parsley and lemon juice on top.

Fasolia gigandes me loukanika

Butterbeans with sausages

Ingredients for 6 persons

(Epirus)

1 kilo butterbeans
3-4 village sausages
1 finely chopped leek
2-3 spring onions finely
  chopped
250 gr. goat's cheese
  (Kefalotyri)
2-3 tomatoes
200 gr. olive oil
salt, pepper

Soak the beans in water for 12-14 hours. Boil them in salted water for one and a half hours, strain, and place them in a small baking tin. Add the leek, the onions and the finely chopped tomatoes, the sliced sausage, and the cheese, cut into small cubes. Finally, pour over the olive oil, season with salt and pepper and cook on a low heat in the oven for forty to fifty minutes.

Salingaria me maratho

Snails with fennel

Ingredients for 4 persons

1 kilo snails

2 onions

2 tomatoes

1 small bunch of fennel chopped

1 teacup olive oil

salt, pepper

Place the snails in water for 10 hours. Throw away the water and drop the snails into fresh boiling water for 10 minutes. Rinse and drain. Fry the onions in hot oil, until they become transparent, add the snails, the tomatoes, salt, pepper and a little water. As soon as it starts boiling, add the fennel and simmer for 50 minutes. Serve slightly warm (not hot.)

Stridia me fresko lemoni

Oysters with fresh lemon

Fresh and clean oysters served in their shells are a delicious appetizer. Open the fresh oysters with a special knife and squeeze on fresh lemon juice.

Salads

Salata horiatiki

Village salad

(Attiki)

Ingredients for 4 persons

4 firm tomatoes
1 fresh cucumber
2 green peppers
1 onion
12 black olives
200 gr. Feta cheese
oregano, parsley
6 tablespoons oil
2-3 tablespoons vinegar
salt, pepper

Slice the tomatoes, the cucumber and the onion, cut the green peppers into rings and place in a salad bowl. On top add the Feta cheese, oregano, parsley, and olives. Beat the oil and vinegar, add salt and pepper and pour over the salad.

Salata aggouri - domata me rigani

Cucumber - tomato salad with oregano

(Mesolongi)

Ingredients for 4 persons

2-3 cucumbers
½ kilo firm tomatoes
2 dessertspoons oregano
1 dessertspoon parsley
  chopped
2 dessertspoons vinegar
2-3 dessertspoons oil
salt

Peel the cucumbers and wash the tomatoes well. Cut them into thin round slices and add the parsley and oregano. Beat the oil and vinegar and pour over the salad, sprinkle with salt and serve cold.

Village salad, top right
Cucumber - tomato salad, bottom right
Lettuce salad, centre left

Salata marouli

Lettuce salad

Ingredients for 4 persons

(Chalkis)

2-3 lettuces
3-4 spring onions
1 small bunch of dill
2-3 tablespoons oil
1 tablespoon vinegar
salt, pepper

Wash and chop finely the ingredients and leave to drain well in a colander. Place in a salad bowl and toss with the beaten oil and vinegar, seasoned with the salt and pepper desired.

Salata apo piperies

Red pepper salad

Ingredients for 4 to 6 persons

(Florina)

1 kilo red peppers
2-4 cloves of garlic sliced
a small bunch of parsley finely
 chopped
oil, vinegar
salt, pepper

Wash the peppers and bake in the oven at 220° C. When the outside begins to blacken, turn them over and leave to cool. Remove the cores and seeds and the skin. Place on a plate or in a salad bowl, add the garlic, parsley, salt and pepper. Pour over the beaten oil and vinegar and serve.

Red pepper salad, bottom right
Cabbage and carrot salad, top left

Salata me lahano kai karoto

Cabbage and carrot salad

Ingredients for 6 persons

(Central Greece)

3-4 carrots

1 medium sized cabbage

15 black olives

2-3 dessertspoons parsley finely chopped

1-2 lemons (juice)

olive oil

salt, pepper

Cut the cabbage finely and grate the carrots. Add the parsley, olives, salt and pepper. Beat the olive oil with the lemon juice and toss the salad well. Garnish with sprigs of parsley.

Patatosalata

Potato salad

Ingredients for 4 persons

500 gr. potatoes
2 spring onions, finely
chopped
1 onion sliced
juice of 2 lemons
1 small bunch of parsley,
finely chopped
1 teacup olive oil
vinegar
salt, pepper

Boil the potatoes in salted water and vinegar for about 40-50 minutes. Remove the skins and cut into slices. Put into a salad bowl, add the other ingredients, and pour over the beaten oil and vinegar. Serve on top of lettuce leaves.

Tzatziki

Cucumber dip

Ingredients for 6 persons

1 kilo strained yoghourt
4-6 cloves of garlic
2 fresh cucumbers
1 small bunch of dill
5 dessertspoons oil
2-3 dessertspoons vinegar
salt, pepper

Put the yoghourt in a bowl. Grate the cucumber and leave to drain very well in a colander. Grate the garlic and chop the dill finely. Mix the ingredients together and slowly, alternately, add the oil and vinegar. Add the salt and pepper, taste to correct the seasoning, and serve cool.

Potato salad, top right
Cucumber dip, centre left
Aubergine salad with feta cheese, bottom right

Melitzanosalata me feta

Ingredients for 4 persons

- *4-5 aubergines*
- *2-3 red tomatoes*
- *2-3 lemons (juice)*
- *2-3 tablespoons parsley finely chopped*
- *1 onion*
- *1 teacup oil*
- *200 gr. Feta cheese grated*

Aubergine salad with feta cheese

(Aigion)

Prick the aubergines with a skewer and bake in the oven for 60 minutes. Leave to cool, remove the pulp with a teaspoon, chop finely and drain. Add the drained tomatoes, the grated onion, lemon juice, and the other ingredients, finally add the oil gradually. Place in the refrigerator for 2-3 hours before serving.

Salata me pligouri

Ingredients for 4 persons

- *1 teacup wheat germ*
- *2-3 tomatoes*
- *2 onions*
- *1 green pepper*
- *1 small bunch of parsley finely chopped*
- *2-3 tablespoons oil*
- *2-3 teaspoons vinegar*
- *salt and pepper*

Wheat germ salad

(Larissa)

Soak the wheat overnight and the next day strain well. Cut the vegetables into cubes and small pieces and mix with the wheat germ. Beat the oil and vinegar together, add the salt and pepper and toss the salad before serving.

Salata pandzaria

Beetroot salad

Ingredients for 4 persons

(Samos)

1 kilo beetroots
4-5 dessertspoons vinegar
4 dessertspoons olive oil
salt

Remove the leaves from the roots and wash both well. Boil the roots in water to which you have added salt and vinegar, for approximately 35 minutes, then add the leaves for approximately 15 minutes. Drain and cut into pieces, toss with oil and vinegar or if you prefer, serve with a garlic sauce.

Skordalia

Garlic sauce

Ingredients for 4 persons

(Zakinthos)

500 gr. potatoes
1 teacup oil
5 cloves of garlic
2-3 tablespoons vinegar
salt and pepper

Peel and boil the potatoes in plenty of salted water for approximately 30-35 minutes. Drain and mash into a fine purée. In a wooden mortar, pound the garlic with a little salt and a little oil until it becomes creamy. Gradually add the potatoes, the mixed oil and vinegar, and season with salt and pepper stirring continuously. Serve cold with fried fish, and boiled of fried vegetables (courgettes-potatoes-aubergines)

Soups

Psarosoupa avgolemono

Fish soup with egg and lemon

Ingredients for 6 persons

(Cyclades)

1 sea bass 600 gr.
6 teacups fish stock
2 teacups rice
2-3 eggs
1-2 lemons
salt, pepper

Boil the fish, remove and keep warm. Add the rice to the fish stock and boil for 20 minutes. Season with salt and take the pan off the heat. Beat the eggs and slowly add the lemon juice, and whilst beating continuously, gradually add some fish stock. Stir the stock and pour in the egg and lemon mixture. Serve at once with pieces of fish.

Kritharaki soup

Barley shaped pasta soup

Ingredients for 6 persons

(Arta)

1 teacup barley shaped pasta
    (kritharaki)
250 gr. tomatoes
1 small coffee cup of oil
5-6 teacups water or meat
    stock
1 sprig of celery
parsley finely chopped
salt, pepper

Boil all the ingredients except the pasta in a pan for 40 minutes, puree the vegetables and return to the pan. Add the pasta and simmer gently for 10-15 minutes. Serve the soup with finely chopped parsley.

Boiled fish, top right
Fish soup with egg and lemon, bottom
Barley-shaped pasta soup

Soupa fasolia

Bean soup

Ingredients for 8 persons

(Kastoria)

600 gr. dried beans
2 medium finely chopped
tomatoes
2 medium carrots chopped
into rounds
2 finely chopped onions
1 teacup oil
1-2 sprigs celery
salt, pepper

Soak the beans in water overnight. The next day drain and put them into a pan with 8 teacups of cold tap water. Add the vegetables and boil for approximately 1 hour. Just before they finish cooking, add the oil, salt and pepper.

Soupa revithia

Chickpea soup

Ingredients for 6 persons

(Epirus)

500 gr. chickpeas
3-4 finely chopped onions
2 level tablespoons
bicarbonate of soda
½ teacup oil
1-2 lemons
dill
salt, pepper

Soak the chickpeas in water overnight. The next day strain and rub and mix them well with the bicarbonate of soda. Rinse with plenty of water and put in a pan with cold water, add the onions. When they start to boil remove the froth. Simmer the chickpeas for two hours until they soften. Finally add the oil, salt and pepper and boil for a few more minutes. Serve with lemon.

Bean soup, top centre
Chickpea soup, top right
Lentil soup, bottom right

Soupa fakes

Lentil soup

Ingredients for 6 persons

(Florina)

500 gr. lentils
1 medium onion sliced
2-3 cloves garlic sliced
2-3 tomatoes finely chopped
1-2 bay leaves
1 sprig rosemary
oil, vinegar
salt, pepper

Clean the lentils, wash and leave to soak in warm water for two hours. Strain and put in a pan with 5-6 teacups of water. Add the vegetables and boil for approximately one hour. Add the oil and the vinegar and simmer for another 15 minutes.

Fish and vegetable soup

2 kilos mixed fish
½ kilo onions
½ kilo tomatoes
1 teacup oil
2-3 carrots
10 teacups water
1 sprig of celery
1 dessertspoon salt

Clean and wash the fish. Skin and remove the seeds of the tomatoes and dice into cubes. Slice the other vegetables and place together with the tomatoes in a pan with water and boil for 45 minutes. Add the fish and simmer gently for a further 15 minutes. Pass all the ingredients through a fine sieve to remove the fish bones, and in order to make a thick soup. If desired you can add pieces of lobster and shrimps and simmer for a further 15-20 minutes. Serve the soup with fried croûtons.

Fish and vegetable soup

Mayeiritsa

Traditional easter soup

Ingredients for 6-8 persons

1 lamb's liver
200 gr. lamb's intestine
4-5 spring onions
1 teacup rice
3-4 eggs
1 lettuce finely chopped
1 small bunch of dill
1-2 lemons
½ teacup oil

Wash the liver and intestines and drain. Boil in plenty of water for almost 40 minutes, removing the froth. Remove from the pan, retain the stock, and chop into small pieces. Cut the spring onions finely and fry in oil, add the intestines and liver and the scalded lettuce. Place in the stock in the pan and boil for half an hour. Add the rice and simmer for another 15 minutes. Beat the egg yolks and whilst still beating gradually add the lemon juice, then slowly add some stock from the pan. Tip this mixture into the stock whilst stirring and continue to stir for one or two minutes, do not allow the soup to boil. Serve immediately with finely chopped dill.

Tahinosoupa

Ground sesame soup

Ingredients for 4 persons

(Macedonia)

6 teacups of water
1 teacup ground sesame
1-2 lemons (juice)
½ teacup barley-shaped pasta
2 teaspoons salt
white pepper

Boil the water in a pan and add the pasta with the salt, and boil for approximately 10 minutes. Beat the sesame, gradually adding half a teacup of water. Take the pan with the pasta off the heat and whilst stirring continuously, add the sesame. Add the lemon juice and the white pepper.

Frumenty soup with onions

Trahanosoupa me kremidi

Frumenty soup with onions

Ingredients for 6 persons

(Peloponnese)

8 teacups water or meat stock
1 teacup frumenty
1 onion
1 tablespoon oil
a little grated Feta cheese
salt and pepper

Boil 8 teacups of water or meat stock, add the frumenty, a little salt and pepper and simmer for 30 minutes. Fry the sliced onion in a tablespoon of oil and add the fried onion and the oil to the soup. Serve with a little grated cheese.

Eggs

Omeleta horiatiki

Village omelette

Ingredients for 4 persons

(Arcadia)

8 eggs
2 courgettes sliced
1 potato sliced
1 pepper cut into rings
1 village sausage cut into
   rounds
400 gr. Feta cheese grated
1 teacup melted butter
1 teacup milk
dill
salt, pepper

Fry in the melted butter each vegetable separately. Put the remaining butter into the frying pan to heat and beat the eggs with the milk. Pour them into the frying pan together with the fried vegetables, the sausage and the Feta. Turn the omelette, cooking for 3-4 minutes on each side. Serve hot with dill.

Omeletta me kremidia kai piperies

Omelette with onions and peppers

Ingredients for 4 persons

8 eggs
2-3 onions sliced
1-2 peppers cut into rings
200 gr. oil
mint
salt, pepper

Put the oil in the frying pan and fry the peppers and the onions. Beat the eggs and pour into the frying pan. Turn the omelette over. Lower the heat and leave to cook. Serve with mint leaves.

Village omelette, bottom left
Potato omelette, top right

Omeleta me patates

Potato omelette

Ingredients for 4 persons

(Larissa)

8 eggs
400 gr. potatoes, cut for frying
200 gr. oil
salt, pepper

Heat the oil and fry the very thinly cut potatoes. Pour off most of the oil and add the beaten eggs. Mix with a spatula and turn the omelette to cook on both sides. Serve with slices of tomato and onion rings.

Avga matia me kremidia

Fried eggs with onions

Ingredients for 4 persons

(Achaia)

8 eggs
1 teacup oil
4 onions, sliced into rings
parsley
salt, pepper

Fry the onion rings until they become golden brown. Arrange the onions into nests and break an egg into each one. Bake in the oven for 10 minutes and serve with sprigs of parsley.

Avga me melitzanes

Fried eggs with aubergines

Ingredients for 4 persons

(Chania)

3 aubergines
8 eggs
1 teacup oil
salt and coarsely ground
  pepper

Cut the aubergines into rounds 2-3 cms. thick, sprinkle with salt and leave for one hour. Fry the aubergines lightly, leave them to cool a little and make a hole in the center of each aubergine with a teaspoon. Break an egg onto each aubergine and continue to fry. Serve with slices of tomatoe and parsley.

Avga mesa se patates

Baked potatoes with eggs

Ingredients for 4 persons

(Arta)

8 eggs
4 medium sized potatoes
200 gr. butter
coarse salt
coarse pepper

Wash the potatoes unpeeled, wrap in aluminium foil and place in a baking pan with coarse salt for 1-1 ½ hours. When they are ready unwrap, cut the upper part and take out about half the inside of the potato. Mix this with butter and fill the potato again. Break an egg into each half potato. Cook on a moderate oven For 10 minutes. Serve hot with coarsely ground pepper on top.

Avga me piperies kai domates

Eggs with green peppers and tomatoes

Ingredients for 6 persons

(Argos)

12 eggs
2-3 red tomatoes
1-2 green peppers
1 teacup oil
salt, pepper

Cut the tomatoes into thick slices and the peppers into rings. Place them in a small baking tin (the tomatoes below and the pepper rings above) and break an egg on top of each pepper ring, taking care not to break the yolks. Cook on a moderate oven for 15 minutes. Serve hot.

Baked potatoes with eggs, right
Eggs with green peppers and tomatoes, bottom left ▶

Avga me spanaki

Eggs with spinach

Ingredients for 4 persons

(Marathon)

8 eggs
½ kilo spinach
2-3 spring onions
1 small bunch dill
1 teacup oil
salt

Wash and coarsely cut the spinach and boil for 15 minutes, and strain. Heat the oil and add the strained spinach, the sliced spring onions, dill and salt and cook for 10-15 minutes. Place the spinach mixture in a clay pot, break the eggs on top and cook on a moderate oven for 5-8 minutes. Serve hot.

Avga matia me trahana

Fried eggs with frumenty

Ingredients for 4 persons

(Preveza)

8 eggs
300 gr. boiled frumenty
2-3 dessertspoons fresh
  butter
8 tomatoes
salt, pepper

Boil the frumenty. Scoop out the pulp from the tomatoes and fill with the frumenty. Fry the eggs in the butter and put them on the tomatoes on top of the frumenty. Serve hot on top of fried bread.

Fried eggs with frumenty, left
Eggs with tomatoes, green pepper and feta cheese, bottom right

Avga kayiana

Ingredients for 4 persons

8 eggs
3-4 ripe tomatoes finely diced
100 gr. grated Feta
2-3 tablespoons milk
1 green pepper
1-2 tablespoons oil
oregano
salt, pepper

Eggs with tomatoes, green pepper and feta cheese

(Corinth)

Put the oil in the frying pan and fry the tomatoes and the pepper for 10 minutes. Beat the eggs with the milk and add to the frying pan, as well as the grated Feta, stirring with a wooden spoon. Cook all the ingredients without allowing them to become dry. Add the salt, pepper and oregano and serve on slices of bread.

Pasta and Mince

Rizi
me hortarika

Ingredients for 6 persons

400 gr. rice
200 gr. vegetables
  (e.g. carrots, peas,
  green beans, corn)
1 lemon (juice)
1 teacup butter
salt, pepper

Rice with vegetables

(Rhodes)

Boil the rice in salted water with the lemon juice for about 15 minutes. Cut the vegetables into cubes, boil and afterwards lightly fry in butter. Mix the vegetables with the rice and place in a mould. Turn the mould upside down on a serving dish and leave it like this for about 10 minutes. Remove the mould and serve.

Rizi
me thalassina

Ingredients for 6 persons

500 gr. rice
200 gr. mussels
200 gr. shrimps
2 onions sliced into rings
2 ripe tomatoes finely
  chopped
3 tablespoons oil
ouzo (½ wineglass)
salt, pepper

Rice with sea-food

(Kalimnos)

Fry the onions in hot oil until golden brown, add the sea-food (well washed) and the tomatoes. Boil for 10 minutes and pour in the ouzo. Add the rice with the correct amount of water (1 teacup of rice to 2 teacups of water) and continue cooking for another 15-20 minutes.

Rice with vegetables, top left
Rice with sea-food, bottom right

Spanakorizo

Spinach with rice

Ingredients for 6 persons

(Kalamata)

½ *kilo spinach*
½ *teacup oil*
1 teacup rice
3-4 spring onions
1 lemon
dill
salt, pepper

Clean and wash the spinach, wilt, drain and cut thickly. In the oil, fry the finely chopped spring onions. Add the spinach, dill, rice, water and seasoning. Simmer for 20-25 minutes. Serve with lemons, cut into quarters.

Lahanorizo

Cabbage with rice

Ingredients for 6 persons

(Attiki)

1 medium cabbage
1 teacup rice
1 onion (finely chopped)
2-3 tomatoes (finely chopped)
2-3 tablespoons oil
parsley
salt, pepper

Chop the cabbage finely. In a pan, on a low heat, fry the onion lightly, add the cabbage and wilt. Put the tomatoes and water into the pan and as soon as it comes to the boil, add the rice, parsley, and the salt and pepper. Continue to cook until there is a little juice left. Serve with sliced lemon.

Spinach with rice, top right
Cabbage with rice, bottom left

Stuffed tomatoes and peppers

8 ripe tomatoes
8 peppers
1 teacup oil
2 teacups rice
1 small bunch parsley and
** mint**
1 onion (finely chopped)
salt, pepper, sugar
currants, pine nuts

Wash the tomatoes and peppers. Slice the top off (around the stalk end). Remove the pulp with a teaspoon and sprinkle the insides with a little sugar. Heat half the oil in a frying pan and fry the onions. Stir in the rice. Add most of the tomato pulp, parsley, mint, salt, pepper, currants and pine nuts. Simmer in a covered saucepan for about 10 minutes. Fill the tomatoes and peppers with the stuffing, replace the lids and pour over the remaining oil beaten with a little of the remaining tomato pulp. Cook in a moderate oven for approximately 50 minutes, basting occasionally with the sauce.

Stuffed tomatoes and peppers

Sfougato

Ingredients for 6 persons

500 gr. minced beef
1 kilo small courgettes
2-3 onions (finely chopped)
2-3 tablespoons fresh butter
6 eggs
parsley, dill
salt, pepper

Minced beef with courgettes

(Rhodes)

Sauté the onions in the butter and add the minced beef. Stir well and mix in the courgettes, (cut very finely or grated), the parsley, dill, salt, pepper and a little hot water. Cook for 30 minutes. Add the beaten eggs. Coat a baking pan with butter, put in the mixture and bake for approximately 20 minutes until golden brown and the surface is firm.

Pastitsio me prasa

Ingredients for 8 persons

500 gr. leeks
500 gr. thick macaroni
500 gr. red tomatoes
4 eggs
100 gr. grated cheese
1 teacup butter
salt, pepper

Macaroni with leeks

(Kastoria)

Boil the macaroni in salted water and when ready strain, add the butter, and half the cheese. Place half the macaroni in a small baking pan. Clean, wash and cut the leeks and fry in butter. Add to the baking pan with the macaroni and stir gently. Place on top the sliced tomatoes, the rest of the grated cheese and the remaining macaroni. Beat the eggs and pour over, season with salt and pepper and bake in the oven until it becomes golden brown.

Mousakas melitzanes

Ingredients for 8 persons

1 kilo aubergines
500 gr. courgettes
500 gr. potatoes
500 gr. minced beef
4 eggs
720 gr. milk
150 gr. grated cheese
250 gr. flour
1 clove garlic
2-3 onions
2 tomatoes
salt, pepper, nutmeg
   (optional)
clove (optional)
cinnamon stick (optional)
2 water glasses of oil
100 gr. butter

Minced beef and aubergine pie

(Naxos)

Cut the aubergines and the courgettes horizontally in the middle and slice the potatoes, fry them all lightly. Fry the onions in the oil, add the minced beef, peeled and crushed tomatoes, crushed garlic, cinnamon, clove and the salt and pepper. Stir to mix and cook for 15-20 minutes. Remove from the heat.

To make the sauce, heat the butter in a saucepan, add the flour, stir, and add the milk, cook for 5 minutes. Cool and afterwards add the beaten eggs and the nutmeg.

In an oiled baking pan place in alternate layers potatoes-aubergines-courgettes- followed by a layer of the minced beef mixture. On top of each layer sprinkle some grated cheese. Finally pour the sauce over the whole surface and sprinkle with grated cheese. Cook in a moderate oven for 40-50 minutes.

Macaroni with leeks, left
Minced beef and aubergine pie, right ▶

Keftedes me saltsa domata kai basiliko

Meat balls with tomato sauce and basil

Ingredients for 6 persons

1 kilo minced beef

250 gr. bread without the crust

2-3 onions

1-2 cloves garlic finely chopped

1-2 teacups frying oil

oregano, mint, parsley

salt, pepper

For the tomato sauce

Ingredients

1 kilo ripe tomatoes finely chopped

1 onion finely chopped

1 garlic (sliced)

2 tablespoons oil

1 bay leaf

basil

salt, pepper

Soak the bread in water. Boil the very finely chopped onion and strain. Knead together the minced beef, bread, onions, mint, parsley, oregano, salt, pepper and garlic. Set aside for about an hour. Form into small balls, coat in flour and fry. Serve with tomato sauce and fresh basil.

Tomato sauce: Heat the oil in a pan and cook the onion, garlic and tomatoes for 5 minutes. Add the bay leaf, basil, salt and pepper and cook for a further 10 minutes.

Meat balls with tomato sauce and basil

Rolo me kima

Meat loaf with minced beef

Ingredients for 6 persons

(Mitilini)

500 gr. minced beef
1 medium onion
2 eggs
1 teacup bread crumbs
1 teacup melted butter
1 small bunch of parsley
1 clove garlic
1 small glass red wine
1 teaspoon cumin
salt, pepper

Mix all the ingredients together well and enclose in a piece of greaseproof paper. Press the corners to seal all the mixture in, and brush the paper with oil. Cook in a hot oven for 40 minutes. If so desired, you can add tomato juice, a little water and 2-3 cloves of garlic. Serve with the thickened juice poured over the meat loaf. Before enclosing the mixture in the paper, we can add in the meat loaf (lengthwise) 3 hard-boiled eggs.

Youvarlakia avgolemono

Boiled meat ball soup

Ingredients for 5 persons

(Chania)

500 gr. minced beef
100 gr. rice
3 eggs
1 teacup flour
2 lemons (juice)
1 teacup bread crumbs
1 onion finely chopped
2-3 tablespoons oil
mint, dill, parsley
salt, pepper

Knead the minced beef, rice, bread crumbs, dill, parsley, mint, onion and the desired salt and pepper. Form the mixture into small balls, roll in the flour and place them in boiling water or stock together with the oil and a little lemon juice and cook for 25-30 minutes. Beat the eggs, and whilst still beating gradually add the remaining lemon juice, then slowly add some stock from the pan. Tip this mixture into the pan with the meat balls whilst stirring and continue to stir for one or two minutes, do not allow the soup to boil. Serve hot with finely chopped dill.

Kolokithakia yemista

Stuffed courgettes

Ingredients for 6 persons

(Langadas)

12 courgettes
250 gr. minced beef
1 teacup rice
2-3 finely chopped onions
1 teacup oil
1 small bunch parsley, dill
2 eggs
2 lemons
mint
salt, pepper

Wash the courgettes, remove the inside, and cut the pulp finely. Cook the pulp, onion, minced beef, parsley, dill, mint and rice whilst stirring. Remove the pan from the heat and stuff the courgettes with the meat mixture. Place the courgettes in a pan with 2-3 glasses of water and cook on a low heat for 40-50 minutes. In a soup plate beat the eggs with a fork and slowly whilst still beating, add the lemon juice, and then slowly add the juice from the pan. Serve the courgettes, with the sauce poured on top.

Lahanodolmades

Stuffed cabbage leaves

Ingredients for 6 persons

(Alexandroupoli)

500 gr. minced beef
1 cabbage
1 medium onion
2 eggs
1 tablespoon flour
½ teacup rice
2 tablespoons dill
1 tablespoon parsley
½ teacup oil
2 lemons (juice)
salt, pepper

Remove the tough stalk and boil the cabbage for about 10 minutes, strain and separate the leaves. Mix the minced beef, rice, onion, dill and parsley. Take a tablespoon of the mixture and place on a cabbage leaf, fold in the two sides and roll up the leaf. Place the stuffed cabbage leaves in rows in a pan, add water or cabbage water and the oil. Simmer gently for approximately an hour, take out the stuffed cabbage leaves and keep warm. Mix the flour with a little cold water and add to the juice that you cooked the dolmades in. Simmer on a low heat to thicken slightly. Remove from the heat. Beat the eggs, slowly add the lemon juice whilst continuing to beat, then add it a little at a time to the cabbage juice. Put the stuffed cabbage leaves on a serving dish and pour over the sauce.

Boiled meat ball soup, top left
Stuffed courgettes, bottom right
Stuffed cabbage leaves, top right ▶

Aginares yemistes

8 artichokes
500 gr. minced beef
1 onion
2 tomatoes
1 glass of white wine
2-3 tablespoons oil
bay leaf, cinnamon, clove
1 lemon (juice)
salt, pepper

For the sauce

4 tablespoons flour
3 tablespoons butter
350 gr. milk
2 eggs
1 teacup grated cheese
nut meg
salt, pepper

Stuffed artichokes

(Crete)

Wash the artichokes, remove the coarse outer leaves and the choke and boil the hearts in water with salt and lemon juice for 20 minutes. Sauté the onions, add the minced beef, the sieved tomatoes, bay leaf, cinnamon, and the clove. Add the wine and simmer to reduce all the liquid. Place the minced beef mixture into the artichokes and prepare the sauce by stirring the milk, flour and butter until it thickens. Add the beaten eggs, salt, pepper, nut meg and grated cheese. Pour the sauce over the minced beef. Place the artichokes in an oiled baking pan and cook for 1 hour at 180°-200° until the sauce becomes a golden brown.

Hilopittes me kefalotiri

Ingredients for 4 persons

500 gr. flour
1 egg
1 teacup milk
½ teacup butter
100 gr. cheese (Kefalotiri)
1-2 tomatoes
salt

Noodles with cheese

(Messinia)

In a bowl, kneed the flour, with the egg and the warmed milk. Roll out into sheets and add a little salt. Set aside to dry. Roll the sheets around the rolling pin and cut into little squares approximately 1 cm. in size. Leave to dry. Fry the tomatoes in the butter, add a little water, as soon as it comes to the boil, add the noodles and boil until the water has been reduced. Sprinkle with grated Kefalotiri cheese and lightly brown in the oven.

Stuffed aubergines ('Little shoes')

Melitzanes papoutsakia

Ingredients for 6 persons

- *3 aubergines*
- *300 gr. minced beef*
- *2-3 ripe tomatoes*
- *2 onions*
- *frying oil*
- *1 teacup oil*
- *1 bay leaf*
- *1 clove garlic*
- *1 small bunch of parsley*
- *grated cheese*
- *salt, pepper*

Stuffed aubergines ("Little shoes")

(Paros)

Cut the aubergines in half lengthwise, remove a little of the inside, sprinkle them with salt and leave in water for a while to remove the bitterness. Drain and fry the aubergines. Fry the onions, add the minced beef, the tomatoes (with the seeds removed), parsley, garlic, bay leaf, salt and pepper, and cook until the liquid has been reduced. Place the aubergines in an oiled baking pan and stuff with the meat. Pour the sauce on top (the same recipe sauce as for stuffed artichokes) and sprinkle with the grated cheese. Bake in the oven at 200° C until they become golden brown on top.

Makaroni kofto me chtapodi

Ingredients for 6 persons

1 kilo octopus
2 ripe tomatoes (finely chopped)
1 onion (finely chopped)
500 gr. cut macaroni
100 gr. olive oil
bay leaf, cinnamon stick
salt, pepper

Cut macaroni with octopus

(Kalimnos)

Wash the octopus (remove the ink bag) and cut into small pieces. Heat the oil in a pan and fry the onions for a few minutes. Add the octopus, the finely chopped tomatoes, salt, pepper, bay leaf, and the cinnamon stick. Pour in 6-7 teacups of water and boil for 50 minutes. Add the cut macaroni and continue cooking for a further 10 minutes. Serve hot.

Makaroni me hortarika

Ingredients for 6 persons

1 kilo spaghetti 'No 6'
100 gr. mushrooms
1-2 peppers
100 gr. cheese (Kefalotiri)
2-3 tablespoons fresh butter
1-2 tomatoes
1 onion
1 clove garlic
basil
salt, pepper

Spaghetti with vegetables

(Attiki)

Heat the butter and fry the sliced vegetables and the finely chopped tomatoes and cook for about 10 minutes. Boil the spaghetti in plenty of salted water, drain and place on a serving plate. Pour over the vegetable sauce and sprinkle with grated cheese.

Makaronia me xini krema

Spaghetti with sour cream

Ingredients for 6 persons

(Preveza)

1 kilo spaghetti (not too thick)
180 gr. sour cream
100 gr. Feta cheese grated
200 gr. Kefalotiri and Mizithra
*   cheese grated*
1 onion (finely chopped
and fried)
salt

Place a good quantity of salted water in a pan and when it comes to the boil, add the spaghetti, cook until it is "al dente" and cool with cold water. Fry the onion well in butter and add the spaghetti, cheese and finally the sour cream. Serve hot.

Makaronia me freskia domata

Spaghetti with fresh tomato sauce

Ingredients for 4 persons

(Argos)

1 kilo ripe tomatoes (finely
*   chopped)*
1 onion (finely chopped)
1 bay leaf
2 dessertspoons oil
600 gr. spaghetti 'No 6'
100 gr. cheese (Kefalotiri,
*   grated)*
garlic (sliced)
basil
salt, pepper

Heat the oil in a pan and cook the onion, garlic and tomatoes for 5 minutes. Add the bay leaf, basil, salt and pepper and cook for a further 10 minutes. Boil the spaghetti in plenty of salted boiling water, cool with cold water and strain. Mix the pasta with the tomato sauce you have prepared. Place on a serving dish and sprinkle grated cheese on top.

Cut macaroni with octopus, top left
Spaghetti with vegetables, top right
Spaghetti with sour cream, bottom left ▶

Dishes cooked with oil and Pies

Kolokithakia
me dyosmo

Ingredients for 6 persons

1 kilo small courgettes
2-3 tomatoes
1-2 cloves of garlic
grated cheese (Mizithra)
mint leaves
frying oil

Courgettes with mint

Wash and cut the courgettes in the middle horizontally. Fry the courgettes and place in a baking pan one next to the other. Pass the tomatoes through a sieve and pour on top of the courgettes, add the grated cheese, the garlic and the torn mint leaves. Cook in a moderate oven for 30 minutes. Serve either hot or warm.

Aginares
me hortarika

Ingredients for 6 persons

12 artichokes
2-3 carrots (thickly cut)
3-4 potatoes (thickly cut)
2-3 spring onions (thickly cut)
2 teacups oil
2-3 tablespoons dill
2-3 lemons
1 tablespoon flour
salt, pepper

Artichokes with vegetables

Clean around the artichokes, remove the coarser outer leaves, and cut off the tips of the remaining leaves. Remove the fuzz. Place them in water with half the lemon juice to avoid them turning black. Lightly sauté the vegetables in oil for a few minutes, add the artichokes, salt and pepper. Beat the remaining lemon juice with some water and the flour and pour into the pan with the artichokes and vegetables. Cover and cook on a low heat for about 1 hour. They can be served hot or cold.

Courgettes with mint, top
Artichokes with vegetables, bottom

Green beans with tomato

1 kilo fresh green beans
500 gr. tomatoes finely
  chopped
2 onions
1 teacup oil
1 pepper
1 small bunch of parsley
2-3 cloves of garlic
salt pepper

Prepare and wash the beans. Add all the ingredients to the pan, stir and add a little water. Cook for 50 minutes, until the liquid has been reduced. Serve hot or warm.

Creen beans with tomato,
top right
Okra with oil, bottom left

Bamies laderes

Okra with oil

(Marathon)

1 kilo okra

3-4 tomatoes finely chopped

2-3 onions finely chopped

1 teacup oil

2-3 tablespoons vinegar

*1 small bunch of parsley finely
   chopped*

salt, pepper

Clean the circle around the upper part of the okra, wash and place in a bowl with vinegar and a little salt for 1 hour. In a pan fry the onions, add the okra and stir. Add the tomatoes, parsley, salt and pepper and enough water to just cover the okra. Cook on a low heat until only the oil remains.

Arakas anixiatikos

Spring peas

Ingredients for 6 persons

(Macedonia)

1 kilo peas

3-4 finely cut spring onions

½ teacup dill finely chopped

½ teacup olive oil

1 lettuce, wilted and finely cut

salt, pepper

Place the oil in a pan and fry the onions for a few minutes. Add the peas, lettuce, dill, salt and pepper and the right proportion of water and stir. Cook for about 50 minutes. Serve either hot or cold.

Patates yiahni

Potatoes cooked with tomatoes

(Evia)

Ingredients for 6 persons

1 kilo potatoes
2 peppers
4 tomatoes
2-3 onions
1 teacup oil
1-2 cloves of garlic
salt, pepper

Peel and wash the potatoes, cut into thick slices, and leave in cold water. Slice all the other vegetables. Place in a baking tin the oil, salt and pepper, the potatoes and the other vegetables, and cover with hot water. Cook in a moderate oven until the surface becomes golden brown.

Melitzanes imam

Aubergines imam

(Asia Minor)

Ingredients for 6 persons

500 gr. long thin aubergines
4 onions
3-4 tomatoes finely chopped
2-3 cloves of grarlic finely
  chopped
2 teacups oil
1 small bunch of parsley finely
  chopped
sugar
salt, pepper

Wash the aubergines and slit from end to end. Sprinkle with salt and leave aside for 1 hour to lose their bitterness. Fry and drain. Fry the onion, garlic, tomatoes and parsley. Stuff the mixture into the slit of the aubergine and place in an oiled baking pan, pour over a little oil and sprinkle them with sugar. Cook in a medium oven for about one hour.

Vegetables cooked in the oven

1 kilo small courgettes

2-3 aubergines

1 kilo potatoes

4 tomatoes

2-3 onions

2 peppers

1-2 carrots

1 teacup oil

*1 small bunch of parsley, mint,
    garlic*

salt, pepper

Clean and wash the vegetables, slice and place in layers in a baking pan. Add the oil, finely chopped parsley, the mint, the garlic, salt and pepper and a little hot water. Cook in a medium oven for 1 hour, until it becomes golden brown on top and the sauce has thickened.

Aubergines imam, top right
Vegetables cooked in the oven,
bottom

Koykia
me anitho

Broad beans with dill

Ingredients for 6 persons

1 kilo dried broad beans
5-6 spring onions
1 bunch of dill finely chopped
1 teacup oil
1 teaspoon sugar
salt, pepper

Wash and drain the broad beans. Slice the onions into rings and fry in the oil. Add the beans, dill, salt and pepper, sugar and hot water to half cover. Boil on a medium heat, until they are tender and remain with the oil. Serve the beans, if desired, with strained yoghourt, or on their own.

Spanaki ladero

Spinach with oil

Ingredients for 6 persons

1 kilo spinach
2-3 spring onions
2-3 tablespoons dill
2-3 tablespoons parsley
1 tomato
1 teacup oil
salt, pepper

Wash and coarsely cut the spinach. In the oil, fry the finely diced onions, add the spinach, the coarsely cut tomato seeded, the parsley, dill and the salt and pepper. Simmer on a low heat for 20-30 minutes, until the liquid has been reduced.

Brocoli with tomato

Brokolo me domata

Brocoli with tomato

Ingredients for 4 persons

(Attiki)

1 medium sized brocoli
3-4 finely chopped tomatoes
2 finely chopped onions
1 teacup oil
salt, pepper

Cut the brocoli into thick pieces having removed the leaves. Fry the onions in the oil over a medium heat. Add the brocoli, the fresh tomatoes, salt and pepper and the right proportion of water. Simmer for 50 minutes. This dish is not served very hot.

Rizopitta

Rice pie

(Parga)

500 gr. rice
500 gr. grated Feta
4 tablespoons melted butter
5 eggs
**6-8 sheets of home-made
   pastry**

Parboil the rice and drain. Add the beaten eggs, the grated cheese, a little butter, salt and pepper, and mix well together. Oil a baking pan and place half the pastry sheets in it, one at a time brushing each layer separately with butter. Add the filling and cover with the remaining layers of pastry, again buttering each sheet. Sprinkle the top sheet with water, and score through the first three or four layers into serving size pieces. Bake in a moderate oven until the top becomes golden brown.

For the home-made pastry

Home-made pastry

4 teacups all purpose flour
2 teacups oil
1 egg
1 teaspoon salt
**1 tablespoon very cold soda
   or a little water**

Sieve the flour and salt into a bowl and rub together with the oil. Sprinkle with soda or water and add the egg. Knead until the pastry becomes smooth and elasticated. If necessary, you can add a little more flour to become firmer. Cover and leave for half an hour. Divide the pastry into 6 or 8 small balls. With a rolling pin roll out each ball separately into very thin pastry. This home-made pastry is used in all the following pie recipes.

Spanakotiropitta

Spinach and cheese pie

Ingredients for 6 persons

(Epirus)

1 kilo spinach
2-3 onions
2-3 leeks
3-4 tablespoons oil
250 gr. Feta cheese grated
2-3 eggs
1 small bunch of dill
6-8 sheets of pastry (see Rice pie recipe)

Wash the spinach thoroughly and cut coarsely. Fry the sliced leeks and onions. Mix the spinach with the Feta cheese, dill and beaten eggs and add the leeks and onions. In a baking pan, layer half the sheets of pastry brushing each one with oil. Put the spinach and cheese mixture in the middle and cover with the remaining sheets of pastry, also brushed with oil. Score through the top layers of the pastry into serving size pieces. Pre-heat the oven at 200° C and bake for 1 hour.

Pitta me koloki-thokorfades

Pie with courgette flowers

Ingredients for 6 persons

(Attiki)

1 kilo courgette flowers
4 eggs
2 teacups crushed toast
200 gr. Feta cheese grated
1 small bunch of mint
3-4 tablespoons oil
6-8 sheets of pastry (see Rice pie recipe)
salt, pepper

Cut the courgette flowers coarsely and mix with the toast bread crumbs, grated Feta, beaten eggs and finely chopped dill. In a baking pan layer half the sheets of pastry, brushing each one with oil, put the courgette mixture in the middle and cover with the remaining sheets of pastry, also brushed with oil. Score through the top layers of the pastry into serving size pieces and cook on a low oven for about 50 minutes.

Spinach pie, left
Pie with courgette flowers, right ▶

Prasopitta

Leek pie (without pastry sheets)

(Florina)

Ingredients for 6 persons

800 gr. leeks
2 teacups corn flour
200 gr. Feta cheese
100 gr. Mizithra (white soft cheese)
1 small bunch of dill
4 eggs
1 teacup olive oil

Wash the leeks well and cut very finely. Sauté in hot oil until they become transparent. Beat the eggs with the flour, cheeses, dill and leeks and season to taste.

Oil and flour a baking pan, put the mixture in, and bake in a low oven for 50 minutes.

Kremmidopitta

Onion pie

(Thebes)

Ingredients for 6 persons

500 gr. onions
1 teacup frumenty
4 eggs
6-8 sheets of pastry (see Rice pie recipe)
2 glasses of milk
3-4 tablespoons oil
mint
salt, pepper

Fry the onion slices in oil until they become golden brown. Heat the milk and boil the frumenty. Mix the frumenty with the onions and set aside. When cool, add the beaten eggs and mint. In an oiled baking pan layer half the pastry sheets, brushing each one with butter, put the frumenty and onion mixture in the middle and cover with the remaining sheets of pastry, buttered. Cook in a moderate oven for 40-50 minutes.

Leek pie, top left
Onion pie, centre right
Cheese pie, bottom left

Tiropitta

Cheese pie

(Parnassos)

Ingredients for 6 persons

1 kilo Feta cheese
500 gr. Kefalograviera cheese
6 eggs
salt, pepper, dill
3 glasses of milk
100 gr. semolina
2-3 teacups butter
6-8 sheets of pastry (see Rice pie recipe)

In a pan cook half the butter and the semolina, until brown, add the milk, stirring, then add both cheeses grated and remove from the heat. Beat the eggs with salt, pepper and chopped dill and add to the cheese mixture. Put half the pastry sheets into an oiled baking pan buttering each one, and leaving the pastry to protrude from the side of the pan. Place the cheese filling in the pan and cover with the remaining pastry sheets, also brushed with butter. Score the cheese pie on top into serving size pieces, and bake in a medium oven until it becomes golden brown.

Pitta me mirodika horta

Pie with aromatic wild vegetables

(Ioannina)

Ingredients for 6 persons

1 ½ kilos various wild vegetables (vrouves, kafkalithres, fennel)
5 spring onions chopped
1 small bunch of dill - parsley finely chopped
3 eggs
2 teacups oil
salt, pepper
4-6 sheets of pastry (see Rice pie recipe)

Sauté the onions, add the washed coarsely cut wild vegetables, and stir. Sprinkle over the dill, parsley, salt and pepper and cook for 15 minutes until the liquid has been reduced. Draw off the heat, leave to cool, then add the beaten eggs. In a baking pan, layer half the sheets of pastry, brushing each one with oil, put the wild vegetable mixture in the middle, and cover with the remaining sheets of pastry, also brushed with oil. Score through the top layers of the pastry into serving size pieces and bake in a moderate oven for 40-50 minutes. Can be served hot or cold.

Pie with aromatic wild vegetables, bottom left
Spaghetti pie, top and bottom rights

Makaronopitta

Spaghetti pie

Ingredients for 6 persons

(Arcadia)

500 gr. thick spaghetti
4 eggs
400 gr. Feta cheese
150 gr. Kefalotiri cheese
4-5 tablespoons butter
salt, pepper
6-8 sheets of pastry (see Rice
   pie recipe)

Boil the spaghetti in salted water, drain and place in a deep bowl. Add the grated cheeses, the beaten eggs, a little butter, salt and pepper. In a baking pan, layer half the pastry sheets, brushing each one with butter, put the spaghetti mixture on top and cover with the remaining sheets of pastry, also buttered. Brush the top with butter, score the spaghetti pie into serving size pieces and bake on 200° C until it becomes golden brown.

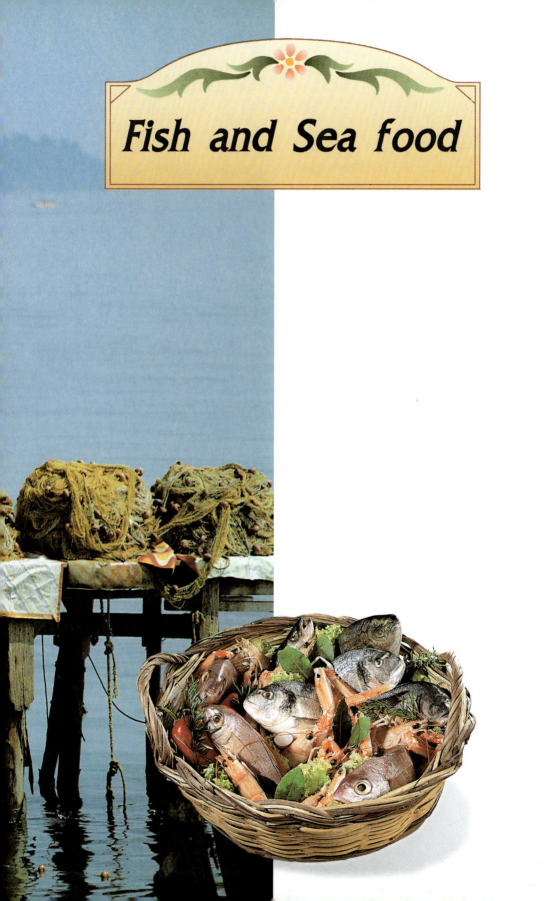

Fish and Sea food

Sinagrida feta ladolemono

Ingredients for 4 persons

4 slices of dentex (800 gr.)
2 lemons
½ teacup oil
parsley
salt, pepper

Slices of dentex with oil and lemon

(Patmos)

Sprinkle the fish steaks with salt, brush them with oil, and cook over charcoal, 5 minutes on each side. Beat the oil and lemon juice with a little salt and pepper and the finely chopped parsley. Pour over the fish and serve with boiled vegetables.

Soupies me spanaki

Ingredients for 4 persons

1 kilo cuttlefish
1 kilo spinach
4 spring onions chopped
1 teacup oil
1 small bunch of fennel chopped
1 tomato
1 glass of white wine
salt, pepper

Cuttlefish with spinach

(Kea or Tzia)

Remove the ink from the cuttlefish and retain. Wash the cuttlefish, take out the bone, drain and cut into slices. Heat the oil in a pan, fry the onion and fennel, add the tomato, the cuttlefish, a little ink and a small amount of water. Simmer for 1 hour on a low heat. Add the chopped and well washed spinach and cook for a further 25 minutes. A few minutes before the cooking time ends, add the salt, pepper and wine.

Slices of dentex with oil and lemon, top
Cuttlefish with spinach, bottom

Bakaliaros vrastos

Boiled cod

Ingredients for 4 persons

1 kilo, approximately
*   fresh cod*
2 carrots
1 sprig of celery leaves
2 potatoes
½ teacup oil
2 courgettes
1 onion
1 ripe tomato
2 lemons
salt, pepper

Clean and wash the cod and season with salt and pepper. Heat the oil, and whilst stirring fry the onion until transparent, add the carrots, courgettes, celery, tomato and some water and cook for 30 minutes. Add the potatoes, lemon juice and the fish and cook for another 15 minutes. Serve with the vegetables.

Bakaliaros tiganitos

Fried cod

Ingredients for 4-6 persons

(Cephalonia)

800 gr. salted cod
1 teacup crushed toast
*   crumbs*
2 teacups milk
2-3 eggs
frying oil

Soak the salted cod in water for 12 hours, changing the water 2-3 times. Drain the cod, remove the skin and place in a wide utensil with the milk. When the milk has been absorbed, beat the eggs. Dip the fish in the egg and afterwards coat in toast crumbs. Fry in hot oil on both sides. Serve with lemon and garlic sauce. (see Skordalia in Salad recipes)

Dolmadakia apo bakaliaro

Stuffed vine leaves with cod

Ingredients for 4 persons

(Kavala)

40 vine leaves
600 gr. salted cod
2 onions
½ teacup oil
1 small bunch of dill
1 small bunch parsley
1 teacup rice
2-3 eggs
2-3 lemons
salt, pepper

Soak the cod in water for 12 hours, (changing the water 2-3 times). Remove the skin and flake the flesh. Fry the onions in oil. Place in a mixing bowl, the cod, rice, dill, parsley, eggs, onions, salt and pepper and combine well. Wilt the wine leaves and place a teaspoon of the cod mixture on each leaf and roll up squeezing the corners. Place the stuffed vine leaves in a round pan, add water and the lemon juice and cook for 1 hour. Serve cold with slices of lemon.

Astakos me freska hortarika

Lobster with fresh vegetables

Ingredients for 6 persons

(Kithira)

1 ½ kilos lobster
3-4 onions
2-3 carrots
2-3 fresh tomatoes
1 small bunch of celery leaves
1 small bunch of dill
1 lemon
1 teacup oil

Boil the lobster in salted water for 20 minutes. Keep aside 2 glasses of the lobster stock. Slice the fillet of lobster. Fry the vegetables with the peeled tomatoes, add the lobster stock and cook for 30 minutes. Arrange the lobster slices on top of the vegetables and serve with lemon wedges.

Lavraki vrasto

Boiled bream

(Alexandroupoli)

1 bream approximately 1 kilo
and 200 gr.
1-2 carrots
1 onion
celery root (celeriac)
1 bay leaf
2 lemons
coarsely ground pepper
salt

Clean and wash the fish. Put some water on to boil and add the vegetables, lemon juice, bay leaf and coarsely ground pepper and cook for 15 minutes. Season the fish with salt and add to the vegetables in the pan and simmer for another 20 minutes. Serve the bream with the vegetables and wedges of lemon.

Sardeles ladorigani

Sardines with oil and oregano

Ingredients for 4 persons

(Preveza)

1 kilo sardines
2-3 cloves of garlic
1 small bunch of parsley
2 lemons
1 teacup oil
oregano
salt, pepper

Clean the sardines and remove the heads. Place the oil in a baking pan and add the finely chopped garlic and parsley and on top the sardines. Beat the lemon juice with the salt, pepper and oregano and pour over the fish. Bake in a hot oven for 20 minutes until they become golden brown. Serve with mint leaves.

Barbounia marinata

Marinated red mullet

Ingredients for 4 persons

(Mykonos)

1 kilo red mullet
½ kilo onions
1 teacup oil
2-3 cloves of garlic
1 small sprig of rosemary
3-4 tomatoes
1 teaspoon red pepper
1 bay leaf
2-3 dessertspoons vinegar
salt

Clean and sprinkle salt on the red mullet. Put some oil in a pan and fry the onions, add the tomatoes, garlic, bay leaf, rosemary and vinegar and cook for 15 minutes. Add a little hot water and the mullets and cook until the fish are ready.

Garides me feta

Shrimps with feta

Ingredients for 4 persons

(Piraeus)

800 gr. medium sized shrimps
250 gr. Feta cheese
2 finely chopped ripe tomatoes
2 cloves of garlic
1 bay leaf
1 finely chopped onion
1 teaspoon sugar
1 teacup oil
salt, pepper

In a pan fry the onions in oil, add the tomatoes, garlic, bay leaf, salt, pepper, sugar and the necessary water. Cook for 20 minutes. Clean the shrimps, place in the sauce and boil for 5 minutes. Put the shrimps with the sauce into a clay pot and lay the Feta cheese, thickly sliced on top. Bake in a very hot oven for 6-8 minutes, and serve immediately.

Marinated red mullet, top left
Shrimps with feta, bottom right ▶

Glosses me lahanika

Ingredients for 4 persons

4 soles (medium size)
1 teacup of butter
2 lemons
2 potatoes
2 courgettes
2 carrots
1 small bunch of dill
salt, pepper

Sole with vegetables

(Cyclades)

Sprinkle the tip of the tail of each fish with salt and rub until you can pull the skin off. With a pair of scissors, cut the fins, and remove the entrails. Wash the soles well and drain.

In a baking pan, place the butter, lemon juice, salt, pepper, and the vegetables sliced finely. Put the fish on top of the vegetables and pour in water to cover. Bake in a slow oven for 35-50 minutes. Serve hot with sprigs of parsley.

Lithrinia me aromatika horta

Ingredients for 4 persons

4 bream (1 kilo and 300 gr.)
2 carrots
1 onion
2 cloves of garlic
½ teacup oil
1 small bunch celery leaves
1 small bunch parsley
1 small bunch fennel
2 lemons
salt, pepper

Bream stuffed with aromatic wild vegetables

(Ionian islands)

Clean the fish, remove the intestines, wash and season with salt and pepper. Stuff the fish with the finely chopped vegetables. Oil a baking pan and bake the fish, basting occasionally with the lemon juice. Garnish with lemon wedges.

Sole with vegetables, top right
Bream stuffed with aromatic herbs, bottom left

Dentex à la spetsiota

Ingredients for 4 persons

1 kilo, approximately, dentex
4 tomatoes chopped
1 small bunch of parsley
  chopped
1 teacup white wine
2 cloves of garlic sliced
2 onions sliced
1 lemon
salt and pepper

Clean, wash and cut the fish into portions. In a baking pan place all the other ingredients and add the fish. Bake in a moderate oven for 20-25 minutes. Serve warm with wedges of lemons and fresh parsley.

Dentex

Gavros me domata

Ingredients for 5 persons

1 kilo (fresh) anchovies
4 cloves of garlic
4 red tomatoes
1 small bunch of parsley
1 teacup oil
salt, pepper

Fresh anchovies with tomatoes

(Zakinthos)

Clean the anchovies, removing the intestines and heads, wash and sprinkle with salt. In an oiled baking pan, lay the fish in rows, and add the other ingredients, finely chopped. Cook in a hot oven for a short time and for 25 minutes on a low oven. Garnish with sprigs of fresh parsley.

Kalamarakia yemista

Ingredients for 6 persons

1 kilo squid
400 gr. rice
2-3 onions
mint
1 tablespoon parsley
2-3 red tomatoes
1 teacup oil
salt, pepper

Stuffed squid

(Lefkada)

Wash the squid thoroughly, remove the bone and the ink bag. In a pan fry the onions in the oil, add the tomatoes, mint, parsley and 2 glasses of water. When boiling, add the rice and cook for 15 minutes. Stuff the squids with the mixture and place in an oiled baking dish, add a little tomato juice and cook in a medium oven for 35 minutes. Served hot or warm.

Fresh anchovies with tomatoes, top
Stuffed squid, bottom

Poultry and Game

Kotopoulo me hilopittes

Chicken with noodles

Ingredients for 6 persons

(Tripoli)

6 portions chicken
500 gr. noodles
3 finely chopped tomatoes
1 teacup grated cheese
  (Kefalotiri)
1 finely chopped onion
1 clove of garlic
1 teacup oil
salt, pepper

Heat the oil in a pan and brown the chicken with the onions. Add the garlic, tomatoes and the required water and boil for 45 minutes. Place the noodles in the pan with the chicken, stir and boil for a further 15 minutes. (The correct ratio is 2 ½ teacups of water to 1 teacup of noodles). Serve the chicken and noodles with grated Kefalotiri cheese.

Kotopoulo yemisto me rizi

Chicken with rice stuffing

Ingredients for 6 persons

(Imbros)

1 chicken
100 gr. vermicelli
1 teacup rice
200 gr. parboiled or roasted
  chestnuts
1 teacup oil
small fried potatoes
1 teacup raisins
1 teacup pine nuts
1 clove garlic
1 finely chopped onion
salt, pepper

In a pan, heat the oil and fry the vermicelli until it becomes golden, add the onion, chestnuts, pine nuts, raisins, rice, fried potatoes and garlic and sauté for 10 minutes. Pour in 2 teacups of water and cook for a frurther 10 minutes. Season the chicken and stuff with the mixture. Sew up the chicken with a needle and thread. Place in a baking pan with oil and a little water, and cook in the oven for 1 ½ hours. Serve hot.

Chicken with noodles, top right
Chicken with rice stuffing, bottom left

Ortikia me rizi

Quails with rice

Ingredients for 6 persons

12 quails
500 gr. rice
2 ripe tomatoes
1 teacup oil
2 onions
2 cloves garlic
cinnamon sticks (optional)
salt, pepper

In a pan, fry the onions in the oil. Having previously washed and thoroughly cleaned the quails, place them in the pan, turning them 10 minutes to brown. Add the tomatoes, garlic, salt and pepper and the required amount of water and cook for 60 minutes. Add the rice and continue cooking for a further 15 minutes. Serve hot.

Kokoras krasatos

Coq-au-vin

Ingredients for 6 persons

6 portions of poultry
100 gr. button onions thickly chopped
100 gr. carrots thickly chopped
100 gr. mushrooms thickly chopped
2 glasses red wine
1 teacup oil
cinnamon, clove
salt, pepper

Heat the oil in a pan and brown the poultry portions for 5-6 minutes, then pour in the wine. Add the vegetables, salt and pepper, cinnamon and clove and a little hot water if necessary. Cook on a medium heat for approximately 1 ½ hours until tender.

Quails with rice, top
Coq au vin, bottom

Kotopoulo me patates

Chicken with potatoes

Ingredients for 4 persons

(Pilion)

1 medium sized chicken
(about 1 kilo)
1 kilo potatoes
2-3 cloves of garlic
rosemary
2 lemons
1 teacup oil
salt, pepper

Clean and remove the excess fat from the chicken, rub with the lemon and season with salt, pepper and rosemary. Clean and cut the potatoes and place in the oiled baking tin. Put the chicken in the middle of the tin and add the required amount of water. Bake in a pre-heated oven for 1 ½ hours.

Kotopoulo lemonato

Chicken with lemon

Ingredients for 6 persons

(Thessaly)

6 portions of chicken
3 teacups rice
2 lemons (juice)
2 medium sized onions
2-3 tablespoons oil
2-3 tablespoons flour
salt, pepper

Heat the oil together with the onions in a pan. Add the floured and seasoned chicken, the lemon juice and 5 teacups of water and cook on a medium heat for 50 minutes. Serve garnished with rice. The correct ratio is 1 teacup of rice to 2 teacups of water.

Kotopoulo me piperies

Chicken with peppers

Ingredients for 4 persons

(Arta)

4 portions of chicken
4-5 peppers
3 ripe tomatoes
1 onion
1 glass of red wine
thyme, salt, pepper

In a pan, heat the oil and brown the chicken for 10 minutes. Add the onions and peppers coarsely chopped and fry, then pour in the wine. Add the tomatoes, thyme, salt and pepper and the necessary water. Simmer the chicken for about 1 ½ hours on a low heat.

Kotopoulo me portokali

Chicken with orange

Ingredients for 4 persons

(Chalkida)

1 chicken about 1 kilo
100 gr. butter
2 onions finely chopped
4 oranges
clove, cinnamon
salt, pepper

Place the butter in a baking pan to heat in the oven and brown the chicken on all sides. Pour in the juice of the 4 oranges, add all the other ingredients and 2 glasses of hot water. Bake on a low heat for 1 ½ hours.

Chicken with peppers, top left
Chicken with orange, bottom right ▶

Lagos stifado

Stewed hare with onions

Ingredients for 6 persons

(Roumeli)

1 hare, about 1 ½ kilos
1 kilo dry button onions,
*   cleaned*
500 gr. tomatoes
4 cloves of garlic
1 wine glass vinegar
200 gr. olive oil
2-3 bay leaves
3-4 cloves
sugar, rosemary
salt, pepper

Cut the hare into portions, brown lightly in the oil and add all the other ingredients and enough water to cover. Cook in a covered pan on a medium heat until the water has reduced, leaving the sauce.

Perdika me domata

Partridge with tomato

Ingredients for 6 persons

(Libousi, Preveza)

6 partridges
2 spring onions finely chopped
2-3 tomatoes finely chopped
cinnamon, clove
2 tablespoons parsley finely
*   chopped*
1 teacup oil
the rind of an orange grated

Clean and wash the partridges well, drain and fry in the oil together with the onions for 10 minutes. Add the tomatoes, parsley, orange rind, cinnamon, clove and the required water and cook on a medium heat for 1 ½ hours. Serve with steamed white rice.

Wild boar with corn

Agriohoiros me kalamboki

Wild boar with corn

Ingredients for 6 persons

(Florina)

1 kilo wild boar
300 gr. corn
2 tomatoes
2 onions
100 gr. olive oil
1 glass red wine
rosemary, cinnamon
salt, pepper

In hot oil, brown the onions with the wild boar, cut into serving portions, then pour in the wine. Add the tomatoes, spice, herb, salt and pepper, the required amount of water and the corn. Cook on a medium heat for about 1 ½ hours.

Kouneli ladorigani

Rabbit

(Crete)

Ingredients for 8 persons

1 rabbit (about 1 ½ kilos)
3 lemons
4 cloves garlic
1 teacup oil
oregano
salt, pepper

Cut the rabbit into portions and sauté in the oil to brown. Pour in the lemon juice, add the garlic, salt and pepper and 2-3 teacups of water. Cook in a slow oven for 1 ½ hours. Before serving, sprinkle with oregano. Preferably served with fried potatoes.

Kouneli me hondro makaroni

Rabbit with thick spaghetti

(Agrinio)

Ingredients for 8 persons

1 rabbit, cut into serving
portions
600 gr. thick spaghetti
2-3 tomatoes
2 onions
grated Mizithra cheese
3 cloves of garlic
1 teacup white wine
1 teacup butter
clove and cinnamon (optional)
salt, pepper

Brown the rabbit and onions in a pan with butter, then pour in the wine. Add the tomatoes, garlic, spices, salt and pepper and some water. Simmer on a low heat for about 1 hour. Boil the spaghetti separately, drain, add some hot butter and serve with the sauce from the rabbit. Serve the rabbit sprinkled with the grated Mizithra cheese.

Rabbit, top left
Rabbit with thick spaghetti, bottom right

Papia me elies

Duck with green olives

Ingredients for 4-6 persons

1 duck

2-3 ripe tomatoes chopped

2 onions chopped

2 glasses of white wine

180 gr. olive oil

250 gr. green olives

2-3 bay leaves

rosemary

salt, pepper

Brown the duck on all sides in hot oil, then pour over the wine. Add the onions, tomatoes, olives, herbs, salt and pepper and the required amount of hot water. Boil for 1 ½ hours until only the sauce remains.

Duck with green olives

Meat

Arnaki me hondra makaronia

Lamb with thick spaghetti

Ingredients for 6 persons

(Ileia)

1 kilo lamb cut into portions
1 kilo thick spaghetti
1 teacup oil
1 teacup grated cheese
2-3 tomatoes
2-3 cloves of garlic
1 glass red wine
2-3 finely chopped onions
salt, pepper

Heat the oil in a pan and brown the onions, add the meat, and stir for 10 minutes, pour in the wine. Add the tomatoes, salt and pepper and the garlic and simmer on a low heat for 1 ½ hours. Boil the spaghetti in salted water. Serve together with the meat, having poured over the sauce and sprinkled with the cheese.

Boutaki arniou me tiri

Leg of lamb with cheese

Ingredients for 6 persons

(Livadia)

1 leg of lamb (1 ½ kilos)
2 onions
180 gr. butter
300 gr. hard cheese
2 cloves of garlic
rosemary, oregano
salt, pepper

Wash the meat and beat lightly. Place the lamb on a piece of aluminium foil and put on top the butter, and the other ingredients cut into cubes (and season). Carefully and tightly wrap up the aluminium foil. Bake in a hot oven for 1 hour.

Lamb with thick spaghetti, top right
Leg of lamb with cheese, bottom

Arnaki me giaourti

Lamb with yoghourt

Ingredients for 6 persons

**1 kilo lamb with the fat
 removed
500 gr. yoghourt
1 teacup butter
dill, mint, garlic
salt, pepper**

Place the butter, a little water, the dill and mint in a baking pan. Wash the meat and add to the pan, bake in a medium oven until well cooked. In a bowl, beat the yoghourt with the salt and pepper and the juice from the baking pan. Pour over the lamb to cover and bake again until it becomes golden brown. Serve with potatoes in their jackets.

Arnaki fricassée

Lamb with vegetables

Ingredients for 6 persons

**1 kilo lamb, cut into portions
3 lettuces
3-4 spring onions finely
 chopped
1 teacup oil
3 eggs
2 tablespoons dill
2 tablespoons flour
2 lemons
salt, pepper**

Warm the oil in a pan and brown the onions, add the lightly floured lamb, salt, pepper and a little water, and boil for 1 ½ hours. Wilt and coarsely cut the lettuce, place it on one side of the pan with the lamb, and sprinkle over the finely chopped dill. Boil for another 20 minutes. To prepare the egg and lemon sauce: In a bowl, beat the egg whites well and in another bowl the yolks, add the yolks to the whites. Add the lemon juice slowly and then the stock from the pan a little at a time, beating continually. Pour the sauce over the meat and vegetables, whilst shaking the pan well.

Arnaki me klimatofila

Lamb with vine leaves

Ingredients for 6 persons

(Mesogeia Attikis)

1 kilo leg of lamb with the bone removed
30 vine leaves
100 gr. Kefalograviera cheese
100 gr. Kefalotiri cheese
4 cloves of garlic
100 gr. butter
3 lemons
white pepper

Wilt the vine leaves in plenty of boiling water with a little lemon juice. Lay the vine leaves on a piece of greasproof paper, put the leg of lamb on top (with the bone removed) and squeeze over the rest of the lemon juice. Add half the butter, the sliced cloves of garlic and the cheese cut into strips. Wrap up in a roll and tie with string. Cook in a medium oven for 1 ½ hours, having added little water and the remaining butter. Serve with potatoes and vegetables.

Katsikaki me hilopittes

Kid with noodles

Ingredients for 6 persons

(Crete)

1 ½ kilo small kid
1 glass white wine
4 cloves of garlic
500 gr. noodles
100 gr. oil
150 gr. grated cheese
lemon peel
oregano
salt, pepper

Cut the meat into serving size portions, brown in the hot oil, and pour in the wine. Add the garlic, oregano, the lemon peel and some water, and cook for 1 hour. Boil the noodles in the meat stock and serve all together sprinkled with grated cheese.

Hirino ladorigani

Pork with oil and oregano

Ingredients for 6 persons

(Arta)

1 kilo pork
2 glasses white wine
120 gr. oil
2 lemons
2 tablespoons oregano
rosemary
salt, pepper

Cut the meat into cubes, fry in the oil to brown and pour in the wine and the lemon juice. Add the other ingredients, cover the pan and cook for 40 minutes. Add some hot water, if needed, and cook until only the sauce is left.

Kid with noodles, top right
Pork with oil and oregano, bottom left

Moscharaki me poure melitzanes

Veal with aubergine purée

Ingredients for 6 persons

(Asia Minor)

1 kilo veal
1 kilo aubergines
4 tomatoes
2 grated onions
2 bay leaves
1 teacup oil
1 teacup milk
2 tablespoons flour
2 tablespoons butter
1 glass white wine
salt, pepper

Sauté the meat and onions in a pan with the oil, then pour in the wine. Add the tomatoes, salt and pepper and the bay leaves and cook for 1 ½ hours. In the oven bake the aubergines in a baking tin for ½ hour. When ready remove and cool. Take off the skins, remove the seeds and mash the pulp with a fork. Warm the milk with the flour and a little butter. When it thickens add the mashed aubergines and cook until it becomes a purée. Serve the veal with its juices and beside the meat the aubergine purée.

Hirino rolo
me kastana

Rolled pork
with chestnuts

Ingredients for 6 persons

(Naousa)

1 ½ kilo pork
(suitable for making into a
  roll)
500 gr. chestnuts
2 glasses white wine
2 onions
2-3 carrots
2 sprigs celery leaves
200 gr. oil
rosemary
salt, pepper

Tie the meat with string on all sides and brown, pour in the wine. Add the vegetables and some water and cook for 2 hours. Twenty minutes before the cooking time ends, add the chestnuts parboiled and peeled. Place the meat on a serving dish and decorate with the vegetables and chestnuts. Pour over the sauce.

Brizoles hirines
me krasi

Pork chops with wine

Ingredients for 6 persons

(Attiki)

6 pork chops
1 teacup butter
1 glass of white wine
2 apples
cinnamon
salt, pepper

In a frying pan, brown the chops in butter on both sides, then pour in the wine. Cut the apples into thick rounds (leaving the skin on but removing the core) and fry in a separate pan until they become golden brown. Add to the chops, and cook gently for 5 minutes, test for seasoning, powder over a little cinnamon and serve.

Rolled pork with chestnuts, top
Pork chops with wine, bottom left ▶

Pastitsada kerkyraiki

Ingredients for 6 persons

1 kilo veal
500 gr. thick spaghetti
6 cloves of garlic
1 teacup grated cheese
1 teacup oil
1 glass of white wine
2 bay leaves
2 onions
2-3 tomatoes
clove, cinnamon
salt, pepper

Veal with spaghetti Corfu style

Make small slits in the meat and stuff with the garlic. Heat the oil and brown the meat together with the onions. Pour the wine and some water over. Add the pulped tomatoes, the herbs (and spices) and cook over a low heat for 2 hours. Boil the spaghetti, serve with the meat and the sauce and sprinkle with grated cheese.

Bodino kotsi me hortarika

Ingredients for 6 persons

6 beef knee and leg bones
   with marrow (1400 gr.)
4-5 potatoes
3 onions
2 peppers
2 lemons
1 small bunch parsley
1 small bunch celery leaves
2-3 carrots
2 bay leaves
salt, pepper

Beef knee bones with vegetables

(Macedonia)

Boil the meat for 15 minutes, skimming the surface. Add the vegetables, apart from the potatoes, and continue to cook for 1 hour. Add the potatoes and cook for a further 15 minutes. Add the oil, lemon juice, salt and pepper. Serve, if desired, with strained yoghourt.

Roast suckling pig with oil and oregano

Gourounopoulo
ladorigani

Roast suckling pig
with oil and oregano

Ingredients for 6 persons

(Ioannina)

1 ½ kilos suckling pig's leg
500 gr. potatoes
3 cloves of garlic
100 gr. oil
2 lemons
oregano
salt, pepper

Peel the potatoes, cut into large pieces and place in a baking pan. Season the meat with salt and pepper, make deep slits and stuff them with the garlic. Pour in the oil and lemon juice and add the oregano. Bake on a moderate oven for 1 hour. Serve hot.

Hirino
me selino

Pork with celery

Ingredients for 6 persons

(Trikala)

1 kilo pork (cut into serving
   size pieces)
600 gr. celery
2 finely chopped onions
2 eggs
3 lemons (juice)
100 gr. oil
dill
salt, pepper

In a pan, brown the meat and onion in the oil. Add 2-3 glasses of water and cook for 1 hour. Scald the celery in boilng salted water, add to the meat and cook for 30 minutes. Prepare the egg and lemon sauce (see Mayeiritsa) by beating the eggs and adding the lemon juice and the stock from the pan slowly. Pour the sauce over the meat and serve with dill.

Hirino
me fasolia

Pork with beans

Ingredients for 6 persons

(Kozani)

1 kilo and 200 gr. pork
600 gr. beans
1 finely chopped onion
2 tomatoes
1 stick of celery
1 teacup oil
salt, pepper

Sauté the meat and onions in a pan with the oil until they become golden brown. Add the tomatoes, celery, salt and pepper and a little water and cook for 1 hour.

Boil the beans separately and strain. When the meat is nearly cooked, add the beans to the pork and cook together for a little more time. Serve hot.

Pork with celery, top left
Pork with beans, bottom right

Moscharaki me melitzanes

Veal with aubergines

Ingredients for 4-6 persons

(Argos)

6 portions of veal
1 kilo aubergines
2 onions
3 tomatoes
3 teacups oil
1 small bunch of parsley
sugar
salt, pepper

Cut the meat into small pieces. Heat the oil in a pan and sauté the meat and onions for 10 minutes. Add the tomatoes, salt, pepper and a little hot water. Boil for 1 ½ hours. Fry the aubergines and place on one side of the pan with the meat. Add the parsley and continue to cook for a further 20 minutes. Serve hot.

Moscharaki giouvetsi

Veal with pasta

Ingredients for 4 persons

(Patras)

1 kilo veal
500 gr. barley-shaped pasta
5-6 tomatoes
1 onion finely chopped
1 clove of garlic finely chopped
200 gr. grated cheese
1 teacup oil
salt, pepper

Wash and cut the veal into serving portions, place in a baking pan and add the tomatoes, onions, garlic, oil, salt and pepper and a little water. Bake in the oven at 250° C for 1 ½ hours, until the meat is golden brown. Turn the veal over, add 3 glasses of hot water and when it begins to boil, add the pasta and cook until there is no water left. Remove from the oven and serve with the grated cheese on top.

Moscharaki me kolokithakia

Veal with courgettes

Ingredients for 6 persons

(Corinth)

1 kilo veal

1 kilo courgettes

2-3 tomatoes

2 onions

1 teacup oil

2 tablespoons mint finely chopped

1 tablespoon parsley finely chopped

salt, pepper

Cut the meat into serving size portions and brown in the oil together with the onions. Add the tomatoes, mint, parsley, salt and pepper and the required water and cook for 40 minutes. Clean the courgettes, cut in half lengthways and fry (lightly) in hot oil. Add to the pan with the meat and cook for a further 30 minutes. Serve hot.

Moscharaki stifado

Veal with onion stew

Ingredients for 6 persons

(Rodopi)

1 kilo veal

1 kilo very small onions

1 teacup vinegar

1 teacup oil

3 ripe tomatoes

2-3 cloves of garlic

1 sprig rosemary, pepper

2-3 bay leaves

salt

Sauté the meat in the oil until golden brown. Add the onions and fry for 5 minutes whilst stirring. Pour in the vinegar. Add the tomatoes, garlic, bay leaves, rosemary, salt and pepper and add the required amount of water. Cook for about 2 hours and until the meat remains with the sauce. Serve hot.

Veal with pasta, bottom left
Veal with courgettes, top
Veal and onion stew, centre right ▶

Sweets

Karidopitta

Walnut pie

Ingredients for 6-8 persons

(Asia Minor)

3 teacups flour
1 teacup butter
1 teacup sugar
1 teacup crushed walnuts
5 eggs
2 tablespoons baking powder
½ teacup milk
grated peel of 1 orange

For the syrup

2 teacups sugar
1 teacup water
1 lemon

Beat the butter with the sugar, add the flour, baking powder, and the eggs, one at a time, the grated orange peel and the milk. Mix well and add the crushed walnuts. Butter and flour a baking pan, place the mixture in and bake on a low oven for 45 minutes. When it has cooled, pour over the syrup (see Baklavas).

Ravani

Ravani

Ingredients for 6 persons

(Constantinople)

2 teacups flour
6 eggs
1 teacup sugar
1 ½ teacups butter
1 teacup semolina
2 teaspoons baking powder
1 teacup orange juice and
*   grated peel*
½ teacup grated almonds

For the syrup

2 teacups sugar
2 teacups water
2 tablespoons brandy

Beat the egg whites stiffly and add half the sugar and the grated almonds. Beat the remaining sugar with the butter and the egg yolks. Add the orange juice and grated peel, semolina, baking powder and flour. Add the egg whites and fold in. Butter a baking pan and sprinkle with some flour. Place the mixture in the pan and cook on a medium oven for 40-45 minutes. As soon as it cools, pour over the syrup (see Baklavas).

Walnut pie, top
Ravani, bottom

Kritika kaltsounia

Kaltsounia

(Kreta)

1 ½ teacups flour
4 eggs
1 teacup sugar
1 teacup oil
1 teacup crushed walnuts
½ teacup honey
1 teaspoon baking powder
icing sugar

Beat the sugar with the eggs for 5 minutes. Add the oil, flour and the baking powder, mix until it becomes a firm pastry. In a bowl, mix the honey and crushed walnuts. Roll out the pastry and cut out round shapes with a glass. Put a teaspoon of the honey and walnuts on each circle and fold over, creating a half moon shape. Place in a buttered baking pan in the oven on a medium heat for 20-30 minutes. Serve covered in icing sugar.

Baklavas

Baklava

(Ioannina)

500 gr. walnuts and almonds
1 teacup sugar
1 teacup butter
1 teaspoon cinnamon
500 gr. baklava pastry sheets

For the syrup

4 teacups sugar
2 teacups water
lemon peel (grated)
1 teaspoon lemon juice
cinnamon stick, clove

Mix the finely chopped walnuts and almonds with the sugar and cinnamon. Butter a baking tin 25X35 cm., brush the melted butter onto the pastry sheets and layer them one at a time, placing some of the mixture on each one. On top place 2 sheets of pastry and score them into serving size pieces. Bake on a low oven for 35 minutes. Pour the syrup over and serve after 2 hours.

To prepare the syrup, boil the sugar, water, lemon juice and grated peel, cinnamon stick and clove for about 10 minutes.

Kadaifi ekmek

(Oriental)

500 gr. kadaifi pastry
1 teacup butter
2 teacups sugar
1 teacup almonds
1 teacup pistachio-nuts
1 teacup water
1 lemon (juice and grated
  peel)

For the cream

1 teacup flour
½ teacup sugar
4 egg yolks
3 teacups milk
300 gr. chantilly
vanilla
glacé cherries

In a buttered pan, place the kadaifi pastry, and pull it open with your fingers. Melt the rest of the butter, and pour over the pastry, sprinkle with a little water and cook in a moderate oven for 1 hour, until it becomes golden brown. Set aside to cool. Boil the water with the sugar, lemon juice and grated rind for 15 minutes and pour over the pastry.

For the cream: Put in a saucepan the flour, sugar, egg yolks and a teacup of milk, beat the mixture. In another pan, bring the remaining milk to the boil and add it to the mixture. Stir in a Bain-Marie until it thickens. Add the vanilla and pour over the pastry. When it has cooled decorate with chantilly, almonds, grated pistachio-nuts and glacé cherries. Leave in the fridge for 1-2 hours and serve.

Melomakarona

Christmas sweets

Ingredients for 12 persons

6 teacups flour
2 teacups oil
1 teacup sugar
1 orange (juice)
1 tablespoon soda
  (bicarbonate)
2 tablespoons cinnamon and
  clove mixed
1 teacup crushed walnuts
1 teacup brandy

For the syrup
2 teacups honey
2 teacups sugar
2 teacups water
1 cinnamon stick

Beat the oil and sugar together for 5 minutes. Add the juice of the orange, brandy, cinnamon, clove, flour and soda. Knead until the dough becomes stiff. Break off pieces of the dough and form into small oblong shapes, enclosing in each one some crushed walnut. Place on an oiled baking tin and bake on a moderate oven for 30 minutes. Remove from the oven and dip into the syrup, which you have ready prepared (see Baklavas), and leave for 1 minute. Remove and drain. Put the sweets on a serving dish and sprinkle chopped walnuts on top.

Diples me karidi kai meli

Diples with walnuts and honey

Ingredients

2 eggs
2 egg yolks
2 tablespoons butter
3 teacups flour
1 orange
3 tablespoons brandy
2 tablespoons sugar
frying oil

Beat together the eggs, egg yolks, butter, sugar, the orange juice, the grated orange rind, and the brandy. Add the flour, and knead into a stiff dough. Set aside in a warm place for about 1 hour. Roll out into sheets and cut into small squares or better still narrow strips which you press in the middle in the shape of ribbons. Fry a few at a time in deep hot oil and as soon as they rise to the surface and become brown, remove. Pour over the honey and chopped walnuts and serve.

Loukoumades politiki

Honey puffs

Ingredients for 6 persons

(Constantinople)

4 teacups all purpose flour
2 teacups warm water
25 gr. yeast
1 teaspoon sugar
1 teaspoon salt
1 kilo oil, 300 gr. honey,
100 gr. grated walnuts

Dissolve the yeast in a bowl with 1 teacup of warm water. Add half the flour and the sugar and beat until it becomes a smooth batter. Cover and leave in a warm place until it rises. Add the remaining water, salt, and the other half of the flour and work until it becomes thick. Put in a warm place again for an hour, so that it doubles in size. Heat the oil, wet a teaspoon and take a small quantity of the batter for each honey puff and fry in the oil. The honey puffs are ready when they swell, rise to the surface and take on a golden brown colour. Serve hot with honey and crushed walnuts.

Christmas sweets, top left
Diples with walnuts and honey, bottom
Honey puffs, top right ▶

Mila psita

Baked apples

Ingredients for 8 persons

(Volos)

8 apples
100 gr. raisins
100 gr. sugar
1 small glass of brandy
100 gr. chopped walnuts
1 tablespoon cinnamon
chantilly cream
cherries

Leave the apples whole, with the skin on, remove the core with the special tool. Mix the walnuts, raisins, sugar and cinnamon. Place the apples in a baking pan, fill the centres with the mixture, add the brandy and shake over a little sugar and cinnamon. Bake in a moderate oven for 45 minutes. Serve with chantilly cream and cherries.

Kourabiedes

Greek butter biscuits

Ingredients for 10 persons

(Aegina)

2 egg yolks
1 kilo flour
1 teacup icing sugar
3 teacups butter
2 tablespoons brandy
2-3 vanilla
2 tablespoons rosewater (at
*   supermarkets and stores of*
*   confectionery supplies)*
1 teacup almonds
1 tablespoon soda

Beat the butter with the sugar, add the egg yolks and beat until the mixture rises. Next add the flour, brandy, vanilla, and almonds, and knead until the dough is soft. Leave for 1 hour. Form into round balls and place on an oiled baking tin and cook on a low oven for 30 minutes. When ready sprinkle with rosewater and coat with icing sugar.

Baked apples, bottom left
Greek butter biscuits, bottom right
Must biscuits, top right

Moustokouloura

Must biscuits

Ingredients for 12 persons

(Attiki)

1 teacup must syrup
1 teacup sugar
1 teacup oil
8 teacups flour
3 tablespoons baking powder
3 tablespoons brandy
1 orange (juice and
   grated rind)
1 teaspoon cinnamon

Mix the sugar with the must syrup, oil, orange juice, grated peel and the brandy. Add the flour, baking powder and cinnamon. Knead well and occasionally add a little flour so that the dough becomes fairly stiff. Form into rounds, place on an oiled baking tin and bake on a moderate oven for 15-18 minutes.

Tiganites me meli

Fritters with honey

Ingredients for 4 persons

(Preveza)

2 eggs
1 ½ teacups flour
2 teaspoons baking powder
3 tablespoons sugar
1 teaspoon oil
2 tablespoons milk
honey
cinnamon

Mix together the flour, sugar, milk, baking powder, oil and the eggs. Beat until the batter becomes smooth. Heat the oil in a frying pan and place in it a few teaspoons at a time of the batter. Fry until they become golden brown on both sides. Serve hot with honey and a mixture of sugar with cinnamon powder, sprinkled on top.

Halvas me simigdali

Halva with semolina

Ingredients for 8 persons

(Constantinople)

1 teacup oil
2 teacups semolina
½ teacup raisins
½ teacup pine nuts

For the syrup
2 ½ teacups sugar
4 teacups water
lemon (grated peel and a little juice)
cinnamon

Cook the semolina in the oil for 5-8 minutes until golden brown. Add the pine nuts and raisins and stir for another 5 minutes. Take off the heat and add the syrup, which should not be very hot (see Baklavas). Return the mixture to the heat and cook for a further 5 minutes. Place in moulds, leave for a little and after turning out, shake over some cinnamon powder.

Svinghi

Ingredients for 6 persons

¹/₃ teacup butter

1 teacup water

2 tablespoons sugar

1 teacup flour

3 eggs

frying oil

orange peel grated

cinnamon

salt

For the syrup

2 teacups sugar

1 teacup water

1 tablespoon lemon juice

Boil the butter, 1 teacup water, 2 tablespoons sugar, salt and grated orange peel. Add the flour and stir continuously with a large wooden spoon. When the mixture becomes a firm dough, remove from the heat and place into a bowl. Set aside for 5 minutes. Add the eggs into the dough, one at a time, beating continuously. Stop beating when the dough becomes glossy and smooth. Put the oil in the frying pan to heat on 180° C. Wet a teaspoon, take a small quantity of the dough for each svinghos and fry in the oil. As soon as the svinghi swell and rise to the surface, and take on a golden brown colour, turn them round. Remove and drain on kitchen paper. Place them in a serving dish, pour over the syrup, which you have ready prepared, and sprinkle with cinnamon. Serve hot.

To prepare the syrup, boil the sugar, water and lemon juice for 10 minutes.

Fritters with honey, right

Halva with semolina, left ▶

Rizogalo

Rice pudding

Ingredients for 6 persons

(Larissa)

1 kilo milk
1 teacup rice
1 teacup sugar
1 tablespoon butter
1 cinnamon stick
2 egg yolks
cinnamon powder

Cook the milk with the sugar and rice until it thickens. Add the egg yolks, cinnamon stick, and the butter. When the mixture begins to set, remove from the heat and divide into bowls, sprinkle the top with cinnamon powder.

Moustalevria

Must-jelly

Ingredients for 6 persons

(Mesogeia)

500 gr. flour
4 tablespoons sesame
1 ½ kilos ready must
powdered cinnamon
pounded walnuts

In a saucepan, mix the flour and must and boil to thicken, stirring continuously to avoid it setting. Pour the must onto plates or in a small bowl and leave to set. Before serving sprinkle with sesame, cinnamon powder and pounded walnuts.

Giaourti me vissino

Yoghourt with sour cherry preserve

Ingredients for 6 persons

(Pilion)

1 kilo strained yoghourt
300 gr. sour cherry preserve
200 gr. crushed walnuts

Put the yoghourt into 6 bowls and place on top the cherry preserve and the crushed walnuts. Serve cold.

Rice pudding, left
Must jelly, top right
Yoghourt with sour cherry preserve

Achladi gliko

Pear preserve (spoon sweet)

Ingredients

(Central Greece)

- *1 kilo small pears*
- *2 lemons*
- *1 kilo sugar*
- *2 ½ teacups water*
- *1 vanilla*
- *2 tablespoons blanched almonds*

Peel the pears and remove the seeds. Place in a pan with the water, lemon juice and sugar and boil until the syrup is set. Add the blanched almonds and the vanilla in the syrup.

Melitzanaki gliko

Small aubergine preserve (spoon sweet)

Ingredients

(Arcadia)

- *1 kilo aubergines (a specific kind of very small aubergines)*
- *2 lemons*
- *6 teacups sugar*
- *3 teacups water*
- *1 ½ teacups honey*

Remove the skins from the aubergines, slit and place in lemon juice for 1 minute to become firm, drain and boil for 20 minutes. Drain again. Bring to the boil the sugar, honey and water, add the aubergines and simmer on a low heat for 20 minutes until the syrup sets.

Kydoni gliko

Quince preserve (spoon sweet)

(Macedonia)

Ingredients

- *1 kilo quince*
- *6 teacups water*
- *lemon juice*
- *2 kilos sugar*
- *1 teaspoon vanilla*
- *10-12 sweet-scented pelargonium leaves*

Clean the quince and grate coarsely on their special grater. Place in a pan with the water and a little lemon juice, and cook until tender. Add the sugar and cook for 15 more minutes. Sprinkle in the vanilla and add the sweet-scented pelargonium leaves.

Vissino gliko

Sour cherry preserve (spoon sweet)

(Volos)

Ingredients

- *1 kilo sour cherries (vissino)*
- *2 teacups water*
- *1 kilo sugar*

Wash and clean the cherries and remove the stones. Place the stones in water and leave for 1 hour to soak. Cook the cherries in the water from the stones, and the sugar for 30 minutes until the preserve has set slightly.

Small auberbine preserve, bottom left
Sour cherry preserve, top right
Cherry preserve, bottom centre
Pergamonto preserve, right ▶

179

Verikoko gliko

Apricot preserve (spoon sweet)

Ingredients

(Naousa)

2 kilos apricots (Kaisia type)
1 kilo sugar
1 teacup glucose
lime water (buy a 300 gr. piece
*   of lime from where they sell*
*   building materials and place*
*   in 1 litre water)*
almonds (blanched)

Remove the skins and stones from the apricots (without opening them). Put the apricots in the lime water for 2 hours. Rinse thoroughly with plenty of water and drain. Boil the sugar and 1 litre water for 15-20 minutes to make a syrup. Cool the syrup and add the apricots. Leave like this for 24 hours. Add the glucose and boil until the syrup is set. Add the blanched almonds in the place of the stones.

Giaourtopitta

Yoghourt pie

Ingredients for 8 persons

(Ioannina)

3 teacups flour
1 teacup yoghourt
1 teacup butter
1 teacup sugar
6 eggs
1 teaspoon baking powder

For the syrup

2 teacups sugar
1 teacup water
lemon (grated peel and juice)

Beat the butter together with the sugar and put in the egg yolks one at a time. Add the flour and baking powder. Beat the whites of the eggs separately and add to the mixture. Add the yoghourt, stirring continuously. Butter a baking pan, place the mixture in, and bake on a medium oven for 40-45 minutes. When it cools pour over the syrup (see Baklavas).

Greek coffee

For a long time, the traditional Greek coffee has been identified with everyday life in Greece. It is made from freshly roasted and freshly ground coffee beans, and prepared in a special little pot called a "briki". The desired type of coffee depends on the way and the time for which it is boiled and the proportions of coffee and sugar.

Traditional Greek coffee, usually served in a small, white, thick cup, remains a firm favourite with Greeks, despite the wide variety of refined coffees available on the market.

Greek Wines

Wine is something we drink every day, and also serve to lend a special flavour to formal dinners.

Vines grow anywhere in Greece, and are one of the country's most successful crops. The variety of the land in which they are cultivated is matched by the variety of grapes and of the taste of the wines produced from them. Whatever part of Greece you visit, it is always worth sampling the local wine and enjoying the particular taste of the region. The best known Greek wines include: **retsina**, a distinctive white wine that should not be allowed to age; **mavrodaphni**, a red wine with a rich taste; **zitsa**, a white or red, semi-sparkling wine produced in Epiros; **robola**, a white whine of Kephalonia; the **verdea** of Zakynthos, the sweet **Samian** wine, and the superb white, rosé, or red, dry or sweet wines of **Chalkidiki**, **Naoussa**, **Santorini**, **Rhodes** and **Nemea**.

Finally, **ouzo**, a drink with a very distinctive taste, is served with "mezedes", as an appetizer.

The ancient Greek god Dionysos was the patron god of wine and fertility - the god who, with the aid of wine and the dance, redeemed men from the cares and troubles of everyday life.

Greek cheeses

Cheese is an indispensible complement to any meal. We are told by the ancient Greek authors that even in ancient times the Greeks practised the art of making cheese. Now as then, people take great delight in the taste of cheese, and consume it in great quantities.

Some of the most famous Greek cheeses are:

Feta, a white cheese, and the one most consumed in Greece. It is made of sheep's milk, and can be soft or fairly hard, with a spicy or slightly sour taste.

Manouri, another soft white cheese made from sheep's milk, containing the full cream. It is very tasty and of superior quality, but it cannot be kept for long and so has to be consumed quickly.

Mizithra, a white cheese, a version of manouri, though of inferior quality and not so fat.

Anthotyro, a kind of soft mizithra either with the full cream or with the cream removed.

Kopanisti, a spicy white cheese suitable for spreading on bread. Served as an appetizer with ouzo or white wine. The kopanisti of Mykonos is famous.

Touloumotyri, a soft white cheese from sheep's or goat's milk, kept in a bag made of the animal's hide. Its taste resembles that of feta.

Graviera, a quality hard yellow cheese, made mainly of cow's milk. It has a sweet taste

and large holes.

Kephalograviera, a hard, whitish yellow cheese made of cow's milk. It has a spicy taste and is full of small holes.

Kephalotyri, a hard whitish yellow cheese with small holes, made from a blend of sheep's and goat's milk. It is salty and has a spicy taste, and is suitable for grating and serving on spaghetti.

Kaseri, a semi-hard whitish yellow cheese, made of sheep's milk, with a slightly spicy taste.

Fruit grown in Greece

In the land of Greece, blessed by the gods, where the sun shines most days of the year, fruit trees flourish and give rich yields noted for their sweet taste, delicate aroma and variety of colour. In addition to being healthy for the diet, fruit thus also satisfies the aesthetic senses, and forms a happy picture, with its wealth of colours and variety of shapes. Oranges, mandarins, pears, honey-dew melons, grapes, water melons, figs, cherries, strawberries,

plums and a host of other kinds of fruit keep us company the whole year round at our daily table and on festive occasions.

Their skin, flesh and pips are also used to produce a number of sweet drinks (liqueurs) and an outstanding range of preserves.

The **olive**, a unique fruit, forms a tasty appetizer and for previous generations was a basic element in the Greek diet. There are many different kinds of olives available on the Greek market, and some select varieties. Olive oil has proved to be a very healthy fat for a natural diet and for cooking.

USEFUL TIPS

1. To prevent artichokes becoming black, wipe them with lemon and place them in water with lemon juice and a little flour.

2. If the food is too salty, cut some slices of potato and boil them in with the food.

3. To facilitate the peeling of chestnuts, make a cut on the outside, place them in a baking pan with a little water and cook on a low heat in the oven for 8 minutes.

4. When boiling cabbage, the unpleasant smell can be reduced by placing a slice of bread wrapped in muslin in the pan.

5. Frozen meat or fish, and frozen vegetables should always be wrapped in greaseproof paper. Defrost the food overnight before cooking. Frozen food should not be put in hot water to defrost as it loses its goodness.

6. To avoid tears when peeling onions, clean them in cold water.

7. To get the juice out of lemons, put them in hot water before squeezing.

8. To avoid getting insects in stored pulses, add a little salt, and shake the bag in which they are kept from time to time.

9. Always stew apples by boiling them in an aluminium pan to avoid the apples becoming black.

10. Put dried peas in water to soften for 24 hours and leave them for another 24 hours without water before cooking, their flavour will resemble fresh peas when cooked.

11. On opening a tin of tomato paste, put the remaining paste in a pot or jar with enough oil to cover the surface of the tomato.

12. To make light omelettes, for each egg add a teaspoon of water or milk.

13. To make the peeling of potatoes easier, place in boiling water for a few minutes.

14. To make rice white and firm, put a teaspoon of lemon juice in the cooking water.

15. Fowl can be kept for many days if you remove the entrails and coat well with melted butter.

16. When melting chocolate, to avoid it sticking to the pan, first coat the pan with butter.

17. When making a cake with currents or dried fruit, to prevent them sinking to the bottom of the cake tin, coat them in flour previously.

18. When food burns do not add water. Place the pan in a bowl of cold water for a few minutes. Afterwards empty the food into another pan.

19. To boil beans, peas, carrots etc. put a little water in the pan and after it comes to the boil, add the vegetables. All the other methods, destroy the vitamins.

20. In order that green vegetables retain their fresh colour a little iodine salt should be added to the water when they boil. This salt can be bought from pharmacies.

21. To freshen stale bread, dip it quickly into water and place in the oven for a few minutes. Serve it hot.

22. Fish should be boiled on a low heat. If you wish to serve it cold leave it to cool in its own juices.

23. Use baking soda to clean stains from an electric enamel cooker.

24. If candle wax falls onto the carpet, tablecloth or any other material, cover with a piece of blotting paper and iron with a hot iron.

25. If red wine spills onto material, pour a lot of ouzo and salt onto the stain.

26. If you spill a liqueur on your clothes, put cold water on the stain to dissolve the sugar and afterwards some white spirit.

27. To clean a meat slicer cut a few slices of thin bread and afterwards wash with cold water.

28. The pith of the orange cleans all leather, and especially calf.

29. When placing a pan on the cooker make sure that the handle is facing towards the wall, in this way there is no danger of the pan falling.

CONVERSIONS TO GRAMS

1 teacup solids: 120-150 gr.
1 teacup liquids: 225-250 gr.
1 small coffeecup: 35-40 gr.
1 tablespoon: 16 gr.
3 teaspoons: 1 tablespoon: 16 gr.
1 glass of water: 130-175 gr.
1 small glass of wine: 65-80 gr.